J. YANCY MERCHANT JR

THIS IS WHY

YOU GO TO COLLEGE

How to successfully graduate in REAL LIFE STUDIES
outside the classroom and beyond...

The ultimate college Survival Guide

Introducing *Merchant's NEW FACE Method for Success*

This publication is carefully compiled from the experience and advice of college graduates who are now successful career driven individuals; business owners, teachers, doctors and lawyers, just to name a few. It's a how-to guide focused on strategies developed to successfully take advantage of the college experience. This will serve as a learning tool to excel outside of the classroom and provide information that you can ultimately master and apply in your daily life.

"There is more to college than just going to class."

Part of the THIS IS WHY series

THIS IS WHY

This publication is designed to provide accurate and authoritative information
in regard to the subject matter covered. It is sold with the understanding that
the publisher is not engaged in rendering legal, accounting or other
professional service. If legal advice or other expert assistance is required, the
services of a competent professional person should be sought-from a declara-
tion of
principles jointly adapted by a committee of the American bar association and
a committee of publishers association.

All brand names and product names used in this book
are trademarks, registered trademarks or trade names of their respective hold-
ers. New Face Management, LLC is not associated with any product or vendor
in this book.

First printing 2019

7528167311 copyright.gov
9781078134620 Paperback ISBN

Published by James Yancy Merchant, Jr
New Face Management, LLC

THIS IS

www.thisiswhydoc.com

Cover design by
Brian Brewer, Ralph Oliver & J. Yancy Merchant, Jr

Editing by
Dr. Kenya Malcolm, Angee Costa, Jessica Washington, Candyce Payton,

THIS IS WHY

TO ALL THOSE TRYING TO DO BETTER IN LIFE, THIS BOOK IS
DEDICATED TO YOU....

"Fingers interlocked ...not one child left behind"

THIS IS

REVIEWS:

"Equally balanced in its informative yet urgent nature, This is Why has as-signed itself the complex task of laying out the foundations of a successful col-lege experience, traversing the multifaceted domains of higher education - from academic and extracurricular to professional and socio-emotional. As put by James Yancy Merchant himself - the book exposes the reader to strategies for succeeding "inside and outside of the classroom." This book achieves that and more by sharing the narratives of former students who come from diverse backgrounds within the African Diaspora - including stories from Merchant himself - that give an honest take on what was and always will be important to overcoming challenges for students of school and students of life. This capti-vating read took little time to read, but much longer to digest because of the rich material and step-by-step guidance that is provided as the book progress-es. As a clinical psychologist and educational consultant, I strongly recom-mend This Is Why for potential students, parents, educators, guidance coun-selors, mentors, coaches, or anyone who has a hand in impacting the life of a current or future student of higher learning."
-Howard Crumpton, Ph.D.
Principal Owner, Licensed Clinical Psychologist
Reach Out Therapy, LLC
Gaithersburg, MD 20878
drhcrumpton@gmail.com

"AFTER reading this book, I wish I could do College all over again. It's truly a methodology that will not only make a student successful IN school, but in life. Each chapter gives a new perspective that shatters paradigms of the past so that ANYONE can use EVERYTHING at their disposal to make the most of their collegiate experience. Most of what is learned and experience in higher education, is outside of the classroom. And 'This is why" gives a formula on HOW to recognize the opportunities for learning, growing profiting and ma-neuvering through the twists and turns of life; giving the students the opportu-nity to take advantage of some of the best years of their lives and be AT LEAST 2 steps ahead of their peers."
-Carl Gray III, Entrepreneur

THIS IS WHY

"This is why is incredibly relatable as a first generation college student I was able to find myself in the book through all of the stories shared making me realize how much more I can do in my own space. High school students please read this book with care and purpose Identifying your goals and actualizing them. This is why is a must read for all High school students especially those who are first generation college students. Unlock the tools! This is why helped me unlock more of mine! This is why is a
MUST READ WITH CARE AND INTENTION!"
-Chelsea Alexander undergraduate student at Hampton University

"Yes, this is why you go to college! This book is necessary, because it will increase college and life readiness for all. Although it's seemingly targeted to only high school and college students, I personally attest that it's for young adult graduates and adults too. The book manages to navigate from college preparation all the way to whole-person and life concepts that add value forever. I was amazed at how it resonated with my past high school and collegiate memories, served as a reminder and refresher of many concepts, and even confirmed my plans and actions as a parent of young children. I implore you to read this book, implement and remember its many recommendations, and pay it forward by living and sharing it! Be blessed and successful!"
- Derrick Taylor, 2006 graduate , Federal Public Sector Manager, and Community Activist

"This is Why by J. Yancy Merchant, Jr is Intriguing, Inspirational, and Insightful. Through the authors college experiences, he shares his achievements and the connections he gained during his time at Hampton University. Through his network he provides the necessities to living a successful life after receiving your college degree"
– Taylor Gribble Undergraduate student at central Michigan

THIS IS

"This Is Why is the perfect embodiment of 'Work Smarter, Not Harder'. I'm so glad that this type of literature is being produced. This is the perfect 'compass' for navigating life 'outside of the classroom'. From cover to cover, I was thoroughly impressed by the amount of knowledge, advice, and transparency that was given and shown. Yancy has knocked it out of the park with this one! "
-Imani J. Dunn, Old Dominion University Alumna

"Yancy Merchant has compiled an essential work that covers the before, during and after of college life. He presents a method for success that is practical and supported by real-life stories from a diverse group of professionals making international impact in their respective industries. This book truly demonstrates that relationships and experiences are often the most valuable component of a successful college tenure and beyond. The advice presented in this work is broad enough for prospective and current college students to apply to a wide variety of personalities and circumstances, while there is a clear focus on HBCU life and the Standard of Excellence that is Hampton University! As a professor and mission-driven communications consultant, I recommend this read for anyone who wants a glimpse of how best to "do college" and those who want to reminisce on this magical time in one's life."
-Erica Taylor Southerland, Ph.D.
www.docsoutherland.com

THIS IS WHY

"This book holds the most important keys to success when it comes to utilizing your degree. The way it sets you up to win even before you walk across the graduation stage is truly invaluable. For current college students, this book teaches you how to use your own talents to recourses to get ahead in life. For those who have graduated, this teaches you how to repurpose your degree no matter how long you've been out. I've found a renewed sense of purpose after reading This Is Why!"
-Stephanie S. Walters, TV Personality & Lifestyle Correspondent

"Even being by his side throughout the journey I honestly always wondered how he did it. I wondered what mysterious personal attribute served as the battery to propel him forward in order to sustain such a high level of productivity. In that regard, the most powerful revelation upon reading this book was discovering that the ability to live so fully and maximize this experience wasn't some unique personal magic that was only available to him, but the fact that it was simply a formula. That may not be as provocative as magic, but it is far more encouraging, for the simple yet powerful fact that the defining characteristic of a formula is that it can be reproduced. The flourish isn't out of your reach, you just need the proper guidelines to get you there. This book is a necessity for the new college student. Don't arrive at the end of your 4 years in college feelings incomplete because you never understood the true reason for being there. This is why."
-Keion McDaniels, spoken word artist and entrepreneur.

THIS IS

Let's Connect!

For information on special sales, networking, speaking events, tutoring sessions contact me below:

www.thisiswhydoc.com

Yancy@newfacemanagement.org

https://twitter.com/newfaceceo

https://instagram.com/newface.swl

https://www.facebook.com/newfaceceo/

Also be sure to youtube and search @newfaceceo to view documentary interviews of all college alumni who assisted in this series!

THIS IS WHY

College Tours

As a part of the **Success Without Limitations** Initiative,

We will be providing college tours for High School Students.

For more information go to www.newfacemangement.org and click on
Success Without Limitations.

Feel free to email successwithoutlimitations2005@gmail.com
for more information.

"Fingers interlocked ...not one child left behind"

THIS IS

PREFACE:

The easy part of your journey is reading the book. The hard part is applying everything in the book to your everyday life. Trust me, it can be done.
The people mentioned in this book are living proof.
Please visit www.thisiswhydoc.com to watch the stories of all the stories of the college students mentioned in this book. Benefit from hearing their experiences. There are over 100 interviews from the
THIS IS WHY YOU GO TO COLLEGE documentary.

THIS IS WHY

Table of Contents

Merchant's New Face Method for Success
9 Keys to be an Effective College Student outside the classroom

THIS IS

Foreword

As a life-long educator I've held a long standing passion for learning, teaching, and helping others to be successful. I taught public school for 10 years, and as a current college professor and author I have the unique opportunity to help other teachers and educators make a difference in their classrooms. In this journey, rarely have I come across someone that is so committed to the success of students, and more importantly, have a plan to help them get to that success.

James Yancy Merchant is a natural leader and born visionary. Knowing his work, dedication, and hustle close to 20 years now I've seen the impact he has on others in magnanimous ways. His positive influence and leadership have allowed him to lead some of the greatest causes to benefit students and community alike.

Now, as an author he has the opportunity to help so many be successful in some of the most critical and defining areas that separate the average from the good, and the good from the great. Lessons on how to not only perform well academically, but thrive outside of the classroom, an area of focus that is all too often left out of the equation.

The implications of success in these areas for students is limitless. Gone are the days where grades alone are enough to carry you from one level to the next. Gone are the days when one could simply "go with the flow" to get by. Success as a high school student, success as a college student, and even success in life is all about how you are able to take those academics and build on those skills to foster relationships, have vision, construct dreams and start movements.

The successful 21st century student is one that is the "new well-rounded". The new well-rounded is someone who has a foundation in the academics, the social-emotional learning and a strong grasp on what it takes to influence self and community for next-level success. This book will give students that blueprint to understand what it takes and how to get there - to be great and successfully graduate in real life studies outside the classroom and beyond.

--

Shaun Woodly, Ph.D.
Speaker, Educator, Author, Staff Development Expert
Website: www.ShaunWoodly.com
www.TeachHustleInspire.com
Email: shaun@shaunwoodly.com

Purpose

The purpose of this book is twofold: to prepare future college students for life-changing events and to give actual real-life examples of people who have vast amounts of generationally relatable experiences. In other words, we have been there and done what new students are preparing to accomplish. The goal is for college students to find success inside the classroom and to flourish outside the classroom by igniting the passion that allows every student to realize their greatest potential.

One of my mottos is "Learn from me...learn from us." It is a principle I have always taught from experience rather than theory. Even before becoming a teacher, I found practical application to be an effective way to convey essential concepts to high school and college students. In the following pages, I will mention specific colleges and universities; but students in any institution can apply these methods. These philosophies and ideas are useful beyond college years and can be applied to your career and life in general. Mentors can use this guide to teach youth the right path to be successful in all of their endeavors.

Each person mentioned in this book attended college. They stem from cities all over the United States. These are true, real-life people and examples–not made up stories. They are all living proof that a mentality of graduating both *inside* and *outside* the classroom gives students the best chance at success.

Every year, high school students contemplate attending college, and many college students consider whether they should stay in school or take a different path. It is helpful to consider college from a new perspective—using a different viewpoint. Consider all the things that happen outside of the classroom and how to use the knowledge you gained in college to navigate those experiences. In so doing, you will use to maximize the impact of your college years. My methods will show you how to take full advantage of college. I will give you tools that will help you excel beyond the classroom by learning from those who already did. Using my *New Face Method for Success* will help you as you pursue your degree but more importantly, you will leave campus with a *degree* in REAL LIFE STUDIES that will help you face and overcome the challenges that await you.

THIS IS

What can you expect?

Let's talk about college. It is a time for learning the power of building relationships. It is a place to establish a network of meaningful connections. It is about discovering yourself. It is one of life's experiences that can help you identify what is important to you and it's the perfect place to execute plans for your success.

I want you to read this book to learn, of course, but I also want to inspire you to teach and spread this knowledge to as many people as possible. I want this to serve as a learning tool for young adults. I didn't write this series to be a one-time read. It is meant to be a continuous resource for high school students, college students, and teachers of LIFE.

Each section begins with a "Person of Inspiration" or a "Featured Business." Each person or business is a part of my network and the *This Is Why* documentary. They are examples of people who went to college and were successful outside of the classroom, which ultimately helped them excel in their careers. Each of these people, though not all famous, is an inspiration because of their dedication which has led to their success. Each section also features quotes and advice from nearly a hundred different college graduates. They took the time to add their perspectives to help make this publication be as powerful as possible. It's important to hear about successful people from the community that aren't on the TV screen.

I have created a method called *Merchant's New Face Method for Success*. This method has been developed through years of direct experience working with people and from listening to and consulting with my peers. If you follow my *New Face Methods* during this phase of your life, you will be more successful in college and after graduating than those who choose just to go to class. After over fifteen years of experience with college students and alumni through my businesses, I am highly confident you will feel more fulfilled while adding value to your degree.

THIS IS WHY

While reading *This Is Why You Go to College* you can expect to read about the different steps to follow past graduation. You will garner the tools needed that my peers and I did not have when we started college. We went in blind. Some of us made the best out of our situation, but we all could have made better decisions had we been more prepared. We have been successful despite our lack of preparation; this has led to our desire to pass on our knowledge to you.

The 10,000 hours
"Put your skills to work"

On average, people waste about 4 to 6 hours a day. That's 28-42 hours a week, 112-168 hours a month, 1,344-2,016 hours a year. Imagine what you could've created if you had used that 2,000 hours productively! College is demanding since it is filled with classes, different organizations you can join, and perhaps a part time job or playing sports. What college life seems to offer little of, believe it or not, is time. Time to be independent, time to do what you want. Time to utilize your skills and achieve greatness! In college, you will have more time than any other period in your life. Being able to manage your time balancing organizations, classes, projects, and fun is essential. It sounds like a lot, but can all be done with proper planning. I always did a good job of managing my time. When people ask me how I balance my days and planning, I say all the time, "I have the same 24 hours as Diddy," and Sean "Diddy" Combs has to be the greatest master at multitasking I have ever seen.

I learned a long time ago that it takes about 10,000 hours to master a skill when combined with talent. Breaking that down in years, you must practice for six to ten years to get great depending on how often you do it and how dedicated you are. That's why I instill in all my children and my mentees to get better daily. If you want to do something, DO IT and be great at it especially if you already found your talent. You can learn the skill.

Deon Merritt who is the owner of Real Skills, a High Intensity Skills program in Queens, New York and played college Division 1 basketball for the University of Richmond and South Alabama University. He spends time in the community encouraging kids to get better and work hard to achieve their goals. He tells his players that basketball can be a ticket to a free education if you work hard. He encourages them to utilize the tools they've been given and use it to their advantage.

If you are not the best test taker and your family isn't wealthy, playing sports and excelling by working on your craft can put you in a position to get that college experience and education for free. Once you get to college, you will be a part of a team that will keep you focused and on task to be successful. Not everyone will become a professional sports players, but you can use sports to pay for your education to do other things in life. Even if your goal is to become

THIS IS WHY

a sports agent, a coach, a doctor, own your own business... sports can help pay for your education. The best things is – you will graduate with zero student loan debt placing you one step ahead of a student who didn't play sports and just went to class. It's not easy though. It takes hard work and dedication.

Now, let's look take a look at the 10,000 hours along with Mr. Merritt's story and apply it to sports, as an example. People with "natural talent" in basketball still need to put in 10,000 hours of work developing their skills. So, whether you are talking about typing, learning how to run a business, practicing law, medicine, or becoming a world-renowned DJ, even someone who is a "natural talent" puts in those hours to be great.

I recommend using the gifts and tools you were born with to pay for your education. You've been developing your talents with hard work; do your due diligence to apply for athletic and academic scholarships. Showcase your talents on the court/field or by competing on academic teams to have the best opportunity to get your education paid for by doing what you do best. Find the university that best fits your talents and skills that will pay for you to get a degree doing what comes natural. Academically, your goal – at a minimum – is to have a 3.0 Grade Point Average (GPA) in high school.

I advise people who play a sport or are involved in performing arts have someone record your games or recitals so that you have footage to send to various schools. This is a visual highlight that showcases your talents. Get familiar with video editing programs like Final cut pro and iMovie. Use outlets like YouTube, Facebook, and Instagram to display your talents. Practice using those editing programs while in high school so that you become proficient with them. Editing footage could also be a source of income to help pay for necessities while in high school and college. Computer Science a major that you may want to consider if editing is something you begin to become proficient in as well. Schools need your talents and may be willing to waive some or all of your tuition. If you dance or play an instrument, there is a school that will pay for you to do what you love everyday in exchange for a college education.

Let's round that 2.7 hours a day to three hours. So, an eighteen year old who wants to be a "master" by the time he is twenty-eight should expect to work on his craft three hours a day every day for ten years. Sound crazy? It doesn't sound crazy to me at all. A productive three hours of daily learning will help you excel. Of course, you will need to have mentors to teach the skills needed and to create a realistic path so that you are learning the right way to do things combined with talent. For example, the medical profession creates a path for doctors to be masters of their craft over a period a time through education and hands on experience.

How much time did you spend in school learning how to read and write? You were taught these things that eventually became second nature. As you continued to learn about reading and writing, you were able to add to your skills. The same applies to sports or anything arena in which you hope to excel. First, you learn the basics, add to it, then you practice, practice, practice. You can adjust the numbers to your specific goals; increase or decrease the hours as age and time allows. But never neglect practice. Nothing in life is given to you. It's earned. Remember that working and playing hard means you need to add in time for rest and recovery.

Using my life as an example, I participated in multiple organizations from the first month I arrived on campus in college. By my second semester, I started an event planning company. During my sophomore year, I had a part-time job and pledged a fraternity. The list of things I did to fill up my time just grew and grew.

Without realizing it, I was spending hours a day learning how to communicate, multi-task and network. I didn't have that natural talent that some people have to play sports, dance or have excellent classroom grades. I figured out early that I was good at various things but not great at any one particular thing. So I was spending hours upon hours, learning people, planning, mentoring, organizing and networking. At this point in my life, I wouldn't call myself a master of a specific craft but I would say, because of the time and dedication I put into those things in totality, I have become very proficient and have success in those areas to the point that I can teach it to anyone.

THIS IS WHY

A major component to my method is planning and having goals while always keeping in mind that it takes roughly 10,000 hours to become a "master of a craft." You have to dedicate yourself to taking the time every day to learn and get better at what you want your craft to be. How does knowing this change the timeline for your goals? Does it change your commitment? Remember, I gave a few examples from sports, to the medical field to networking but you can work on being the master of any craft YOU want.

No matter how old you are, no one knows *you* better than you know yourself. You spend 100% of your life, 24 hours a day, seven days a week working on yourself. You may not realize it, but now is the time to think about what you want and how you can achieve it. Write it down, visualize it, and own it. You've probably had some goals even at a young age. You've probably have plans even if they have changed over time. What charges you up? What gets you to be productive in life? Only you know what motivates you. Think about what you care about on a daily basis. Think about what wakes you up every morning. That is your passion and your drive. Stick to that and let that be the fuel for your success in life. Listen to the advice I am giving you. Listen to the advice and stories of others in this book, and learn from us. I am writing this book after years of success. But it's the failures that have led to the most valuable lessons. It's never 10,000 hours of success! Learn from both so that you can do better moving forward. I want you to be a thousand times more successful than anyone I have ever come across in my own journey. All the others associated with the production of this book feel the same way.

I have spent close to 10,000 hours learning how to network, multi-task, mentor and planning with various people, events and organizations. Now, I have put it into my method for success in this book.

"You miss 100% of the shots you don't take."

Welcome To College

What if I told you your college degree isn't worth much more than the paper it's printed on if all you did to obtain it was go to class and get good grades?

When people think about college, they often focus on the degree they are working toward and forget that there is another side to the college experience. There is a Yin and Yang to it. The Yin and Yang are ancient Chinese principles symbolized by two different colored pieces (representing inseparable opposites) that form a whole to illustrate the contradictory nature of all things. Two opposite natures must work together to form a whole.

If the degree you earn in the classroom is the Yin, you need the Yang to complete the experience. If you only focus on the Yin, you will be unbalanced, unfulfilled, and incomplete. In a sense, the time you spent in college will have been wasted. On the other hand, your degree will be exponentially more valuable if you include tools to help you *graduate* outside the classroom. You will be able to magnify your learning and offer your skills to the marketplace as a full package.

In all honesty, the degree is just the icing on the cake. The most beneficial thing about college are all the moving parts outside the classroom, all the growth that takes place. The degree is the paper that says "I did it."

THIS IS WHY

It's the verification of your success. But that piece of paper will mean so much more if you apply what you learn here.

In a four-year institution, typically students are working on a Bachelor's degree. During that time, you are referred to as an undergraduate student – *undergrad* for short. As an undergrad, I wanted to be successful in everything I did. From my freshman year, I was active in multiple organizations. I wanted to touch every part of campus possible. You will see, that will be the common theme of this book, as well. The set up for success starts early. Have fun, but get active. Even as a freshman, my first year, I started a business with my best friends called Straight Face/New Face Entertainment. Whenever we did anything as the owners of our event planning company, it doesn't feel like a job. It's just fun!

Graduate school is more advanced and comes after the Bachelor's degree has been completed. You may go to Graduate school solely to achieve a Master's degree program, or you may enter a program where you earn a doctorate (e.g., PhD, EdD, etc). I completed a Bachelor's degree and went on to attend Graduate school. I took the opportunity as a graduate student to start a student organization while I also worked on my event planning company and worked as a high school teacher. I was motivated every morning and wanted to get up first thing to teach my students and interns something new while in school myself. It didn't feel like a job. I felt like I had a rich, fulfilled life. That's what you are looking for. You want to work to generate income but not feel like you're working. You want to do something in life that is fun, and you just happen to make money from it.

I have reflected on my time as a young adult and realized that, although many of the choices I made then didn't seem critical at the time, it turned out to be some of the most life-changing decisions I've ever make. Young people are told by parents and other influential adults tell that college is the natural next step after high school. What is college? Is it supposed to be the 13-16th grades? Or is it a place we went just to leave the house where we grew up?

For the student who hates going to classes and/or isn't the best test taker, college could seem like nothing more than four more years of more exams, teachers, and grades. College students know that it is so much more. But how do prospective students get a handle on what college life is like? How would they know that college literally changes your life the minute you move away from your comfortable hometown and step foot on that college campus with bags in your hand into a dorm room? College is certainly not a second high school experience. The life of a college student has officially changed for the better with this book in hand.

College opens opportunities you would never have if you stay in the same place you were in the 12th grade. College gives you the chance to meet people from places you have never been. You can come from Dallas, Texas and meet someone from Queens, New York. You can be a guy from Washington, DC and meet girl from Rancho Cucamonga, California. You will meet people from places you saw on TV and learn that they are just like you. They are confused and excited at the same time about being away from home.

If you were antisocial in high school, you will find that there are just as many antisocial people there; you are not the only one! Now you can be antisocial together! (See what I did there?) Let's say you come from a home where you get everything you want and need. Food is not a problem, transportation is no problem, and on top of everything else, you are the most popular kid in high school. College will show you that - little did you know - there are hundreds of people in the college just like you who were president of their classes and/or star athletes. You will meet students have their own cars, and never missed a meal in their lives. This revelation also happens for someone who did not have all they hoped for in high school, wasn't the star athlete, and didn't have every-one stop the world when you walked the hallways. There are just as many of those people in college like you as well.

College will force you to figure out how to spread twenty dollars over two weeks. It will force you to become an adult and have a blast doing it. College will take you out of that comfort zone called *your family.* It will introduce you to new people who will become a different kind of family. College is necessary change that will force you to mature.

Using my *New Face Method for Success System,* you can easily navigate the transition from your familiar hometown surroundings to the choppy waters of a diverse campus culture. Your ability to learn how to interact, connect and net-work with people "outside the classroom" will prove as valuable to you as the degree you will receive.

THIS IS WHY

You should never forget that the degree is very important. Early in life, I was given great advice by my father, Pablo Porter: "A high school diploma is nothing now-a-days. A Master's degree is proof you can learn a specific craft and a doctorate is proof you can become proficient with a specific craft. A college diploma is proof you can be taught."

Sometimes that proof is good enough to get your foot in the door for an interview. But then what? I'll give you a personal example. I graduated from college in 2005, Cum Laude, with a bachelor's degree in business management. After a year of working as an executive account manager handling wireless services for corporate business, I wanted a change. Along with two of my best friends, Shaun Woodly and Keion McDaniels, I decided to go into the education field as a business teacher. I was hired in Newport News public schools teaching high school business classes. I taught keyboarding, business management, and a few other electives. At the time, I was pursuing a Master's in business administration at a much larger public University in Norfolk,VA -Old Dominion University. I was given provisional status because I did not have a Master's degree in Education. My Bachelor's degree was sufficient to land the teaching position on a temporary status for three years, giving me time to earn my Master's. The Bachelor's degree was proof I could be taught, and the Master's degree was proof I had learned a specific craft.

What I learned outside of the classroom are the skills that helped me excel in my profession. In the above example, the skills were in the education field. But these principles apply to any profession. Even still, the degree is still necessary as proof you can be taught (Yin/Yang). Although I wanted an MBA, I needed to change my major to education in order to keep my position. Everything I learned in college and what I will teach you in this book will help you get in the best positions post college. However, it is imperative to complete at least your Bachelor's degree. In some cases you may need even further "proof" than that whether it is a Master's, law degree, doctorate, etc.

What you'll learn here will teach you how to be above the rest once you get that degree and begin to compete. No matter what anyone told you, life is a business and a competition. There is always someone who wants to be where you are, and there is always a point you want to reach that someone else has tried to get to. You have to wear the proverbial chip on your shoulder and have the confidence that you can achieve anything you put your mind to.

THIS IS

But don't be so cocky that you fail to learn from people and neglect to first do your research on whatever you're attempting to accomplish.

What you learn and how you maneuver and position yourself in college outside the classroom will get you what you want in your career. Trust me, reading this book along with actually following my methods will steer you in the right direction.

Throughout this journey, I will ask you questions for you to think about and discuss with others you know who are going to college. I will give you examples of current students and alumni who have already walked the path and have wisdom to share.

For the adult-motivators reading this who may be looking for answers to give others, I want you to think about your life and explore new and innovative ways to advise students.I encourage you to think about how it felt to be a teenager and how you would have liked to be helped with the important decisions college students have to make.

For teenagers thinking about college or already in college, I want you to open your eyes and see the potential of greatness ahead of you. The world is yours to conquer and this book will add tools for you to use to build your world.

I wrote this book with this question in mind: What would I say if I was able to tell my eighteen-year-old self what to do when it comes to college – if I were to give myself advice based off what I realized later in life. How would I advise someone to with regard to all of the nuances that lead to success in college life: surrounding oneself with the right people, making wise financial decisions, joining particular organizations, balancing time correctly, and identifying their long-term goals. If I could have told millions of eighteen-year-olds what I learned, this book would be the answer. I have laid it out for you. *This Is Why* is a learning mechanism that walks you, step-by-step, to the success you desire.

THIS IS WHY

II. New Student Orientation
Building character creating your adult self

Merchant's New Face Method for Success
9 keys to be an Effective College Student Outside The Classroom

1- IT'S TIME TO SET YOUR SCHEDULE (DAILY ROUTINE)
2- PERFECT THINGS THAT REQUIRE ZERO TALENT
3 - JOIN ORGANIZATIONS
4 - BE THE X FACTOR
5 - BRAND AND INVEST IN YOURSELF
6 - CREATE YOUR N.E.T.W.O.R.K.
7 - DEVELOP YOUR NEW FACE
8 - BE A SERVANT TO THE COMMUNITY
9 -.ALWAYS REMEMBER "WE PROMOTE IT"

THIS IS

KEY #1 IT'S TIME TO SET YOUR SCHEDULE (DAILY ROUTINE)

Inspirational Person Andrew "DJ Babeydrew" Bisnaught
Remember you are in college for a reason
Plan and set Goals
S.M.A.R.T.
Time Management
Take Notes
Prioritize
Multi-Task
Being on time
Adjusting with the times
Surround yourself with good people
Take home notes
Resources

THIS IS WHY

Inspirational person

Andrew "DJ BabeyDrew" Bisnaught

Babey Drew's skills are some of the most sought after among DJs and thus validates his position as one of the top DJs in the world . Based in Atlanta, Drew's humble disk jockey beginnings started in Queens, NY. Since then, he has grown to become a staple in the music and entertainment industry. Drew's DJ sets are both phenomenal, and unparalleled, providing an explosive angle on the current state of music. Drew made a name for himself as the official Touring DJ for Chris Brown, a regular DJ for the Kardashians , and has opened up for numerous artists including Diplo, Calvin Harris, Steve Aoki, Justin Bieber, the Chainsmokers, and more.

Needless to say, Drew's talent extends farther than the tour scene, as he represents Fortune 500 companies such as Microsoft, Nike and the W Hotel. He sells out his own tours worldwide and graves television screens across the globe. His Talents Are limitless but none compare to this mark in the entertainment industry as a world renowned DJ .

Drew's radio tenure is 18 years and counting. He currently appears on power 96.1 in Atlanta, Z104 in Virginia Beach and special guest mixes ok Sirius/XM. His mixes include Electro, trap, Dubstep, Top 40, and dancehall. He has perfect the EDMONTON sub-genre he coins as "Island bass." DJ Babey Drew has found much success since his early touring days. He landed a role on VH1s TV show , and has made appearances on "the Grammys ," "the Oprah Winfrey Show," "MTV's TRL," "The Ellen Degeneres Show," "The view," "The Today Show," "Good Morning America," and more. Drew has performed in over 20 countries expanding his global platform and has produced for an array of artist both foreign and domestic.

He was also awarded a Grammy for his work with Diplo and Skrillex on their "Jack U" project.

THIS IS

Contact :

babeydrewmp3@gmail.com
www.instragram.com/babeydrew
www.djbabeydrew.com

THIS IS WHY

"If your life isn't everything it could be, then what would happen if you stop wasting the opportunities that are in front of you?"

-Jordan Peterson

THIS IS

Remember you are in college for a reason

As I stated plenty of times, this book is to open your eyes to the fact that there is more to your college experience than just sitting in a classroom. The value of your degree will be magnified by the experiences that help you become a more well-rounded individual. Ok so here we are. You are in college, you have now cultivated the intangibles needed to aid you in maximizing the productivity of your daily routine. This particular section is about multi-tasking, time management, and staying focused. Any student who has gone to college can tell you that time is a bit of a paradox. That is to say, you have far more time than you realize, while in the very same instant feeling as though you don't have enough time. The key to not getting lost in this awkward space is prepara- tion. Your goal is to evolve beyond who you were in high school, and to be successful in that evolution you will need to incorporate a few strategies to keep you on task and on point.

THIS IS WHY

Plan

I will be speaking on planning and having to set goals often throughout this book as they are major components to my method for success. Things are much easier if you have a goal and plan to achieve that goal. I recommended that you write down your goals. What are they? This is the part of my method that will set you up for life. Setting goals, planning and scheduling your day, week, month, Year is what will set you up for success. When setting goals you should develop a plan. Gary Keller author of The ONE THING speaks on GOAL SETTING and lays out great way to plan out your goals: Below is an example

Someday Goal

What is one thing I want to do someday?

5-year goal

Based on my someday goal, what's the ONE thing I can do in the next 5 years?

1 Year Goal

Based on my 5-year goal, what's the one thing I can do this year?

Monthly goal

Based on my 1-year goal, what the ONE thing I can do this month?

Weekly goal

Based on my monthly goal, what's the one thing I can do this week?

Daily Goal

Based on my weekly goal, what's the ONE thing I can do today?

Right Now

Based on my daily goal what's the ONE thing I can do right now?

Another popular way that people set goals for themselves:

S. M. A. R. T. Goals

Specific - state exactly what it is you are trying to achieve
Measurable-How do you know you are heading toward your goal?
Achievable-Is this goal realistic? Do you need assistance from people or re-
sources achieving this goal? What may prevent you from achieving this goal?
Relevant-what does achieving this goal mean to you? What will achieving this
goal do for your life?
Time-Bound-When will you reach your goal?

Time waits for no one. The world waits for no one. You cannot sit around and
wait for your desires to miraculously appear in your lap. Things don't randomly happen, they happen as a consequence of the deeds and actions of those who
assert their will. The point is not to just hope things occur, but to create the
circumstances so that they will occur. That doesn't happen through haphazard
action. You must target and coordinate your efforts. The most effective way to
do this is to develop a plan. Create a plan with short and long-term goals.

Lay out how and when you want to execute the plan. And understanding the
benefits of achieving that goal will make it that much easier. Anything is
achievable with a realistic plan, even the things that seem far-fetched. Sometimes you have to just follow the dream and take a risk. Sometimes you have to
just know what you want and go get it. Planning is vital, but it is meaningless
without execution. You can plan all you want, but at the end of the day, you
have to actually do it!

THIS IS WHY

Time management

During the 10,000 hour section I mentioned that on average,

"people waste about 4-6 hours a day. That's 28-42 hours a week, 112-168 hours a month, 1,344-2,016 hours a year. College is a balancing act and your future can't afford that amount of time being wasted. Being able to balance organizations, classes, homework, and organization events is essential…"

Remember I said: "I have the same 24 hours as Diddy."?

Well According to an article by Courtney Connley www.cnbc.com in September 2017:

"Sean Combs, commonly known as Puff Daddy or Diddy, is an artist and entrepreneur whose business acumen has garnered him a net worth of $820 million, according to Forbes. He owns a stake in the TV network Revolt and is the founder of clothing line Sean John. He also has a lucrative deal with Diageo's Ciroc and a partnership with DeLeon tequila, and co-owns water brand AQUAhydrate with Mark Wahlberg. November 2016, Combs took home an estimated $70 million when Global Brand Groups purchased a stake in his clothing company Sean John, Forbes reports. He still owns a reported 20 percent of the company. In 2016, Combs opened the Capital Preparatory Harlem Charter School, where he and his staff plan to provide young people with early lessons on leadership and success."
According to https://www.combsenterprises.com/sean-combs/

"As the Chairman and CEO of Combs Enterprises, he has a diverse portfolio of businesses and investments covering the music, fashion, fragrance, beverage, marketing, film, television, and media industries with companies such as Bad Boy Worldwide Entertainment Group, Sean John, Combs Wine & Spirits, AQUAhydrate, The Blue Flame Agency, REVOLT Films and REVOLT MEDIA & TV"

I watch Diddy's documentary CAN'T STOP WON'T STOP at least once a month to get motivation for my own documentary. The documentary shows a glimpse of the planning and what it took to bring the reunion of his Bad Boy family for a reunion concert nearly 20 years later. He has always been

THIS IS

someone I admire. Now, I think to myself, "Sean Combs, the mogul, has the same 24 hours as the rest of us." There is no excuse for mismanaging your time when someone like Sean Combs is able to balance all of his endeavors while maintaining a poppin' personal life. He also was a college student at Howard University, an HBCU in Washington DC. He did not graduate, but he returned in 2014 to receive an honorary doctorate in humanities and deliver the University's 146th commencement address. He exemplifies what it means to graduate with a degree in real life studies.

It is important to set daily, weekly, monthly and yearly goals. Don't just "know them in your brain," but make the visualization concrete. Some people make vision boards for the year. That is an excellent tool but be sure to actually write them down on paper and develop a plan to achieve these goals. This is way to improve yourself and prepare for success as you grow.

Remember, your goals are things that you are working toward no matter what, even days you don't feel like it. For example, let's say your weekly goals are:

- Workout 3 days a week
- Eat healthy 6 days a week
- Read one book a week
- Learn something new
- Work on your monthly goals
- Save money

THIS IS WHY

For each of these 6 goals, you should break them down further:

- What 3 days will you work out each week and at what time?
- Do you know what it is to eat healthy? What healthy food do you like?
- Pick out the 4 books for the month in advance.
- What is it you want to learn this week?
- What are you monthly goals?
- How much money do you have to set aside each week?

Make a plan for your weekly goals and lay everything out for yourself. Make them easier to achieve.

Take notes

For as long as I can remember, I have had a pen and some sort of pad of paper with me all the time. I still walk around with a *to-do* list. I also use the notepad in my phone. I write notes everywhere. I write thoughts, visions, financial plans, and the names of people who would be great to contact. Sometimes I write ways to make money, ways to make my kids better, ways to change the world.

My grandparents, Barbara and Dean Johnson, told me I always had a plan even as a young child. My grandmother referred back to when I was five years old when I would write down notes. She called it a "supernatural curiosity." I always wanted to know what we were doing and what time we were doing it. I visualized the plan and thought it out in my head. Throughout college, I would plan out each semester. I would sit and look at the events on paper and think about places where it would make sense for me to have events there during certain days of the week and seasons of the year.

Prioritize

I am someone who threw countless parties throughout college, but I also graduated with honors. I also made it a requirement for the interns/street team that
worked with me to have a minimum of a 2.5 GPA. My leaders had to have a
2.75 or higher. You always have to keep in mind that you are in school to obtain that degree so you must balance your time and prioritize your goals.
Everyone has the same 24 hours in the day so limited time doesn't give anyone
an excuse to only focus on getting the degree. That's only half of what being a
successful college student is about.

Do not complain about having no time. Let's break down those hours again.
There are 168 hours in a week. Let's say 40 hours are for class and studying
(yes, it's a full time job)!, 7 hours in the gym, 56 hours sleep. Activate the remaining 65 hours and use the time wisely. I am being very lenient with the
hours. Even if you allocated 10 hours to partying, you still have plenty of time
to do anything you NEED to do. The question is what is it that you want?
Don't waste time. It's your life you are wasting.

Multi tasking

Plenty of sites I have come across frown upon multi-tasking. I, for one, encourage it as long as it's done correctly. I have so many ideas in my head. I
know you do, as well. There are various things I think about doing in my life.
But, I know that – to do them all well – I have to prioritize and attack. Today, I
may work on my book series. Tomorrow, I may work directly with the film
portion of my documentary. Over the weekend, I might work on ideas for my
mentoring organization Success Without Limitations. I have to have an
organized way to keep my mind going and to make sure that the work gets
done. I never want to forget about an idea, so I keep my mind open to work on
various things before that thought is gone. I keep a place to put notes in my
phone.Like I stated earlier, I have always had a notepad that I always keep on
me just in case I need to write something down. I still keep one, in case I can't
get to my phone. Every week, I go over all my notes and my *to-do* lists to
ensure I haven't missed anything. Because I multi tasked so much in college, I
was able to develop 20 events in a semester with my business. I was able to
head multiple organizations, maintain a high GPA, and remain physically
active daily. I was able to do it because of proper planning and minimal
distractions.

THIS IS WHY

Andrew "DJ Babeydrew" Bisnaught from Queens, New York is a 2002 graduate of Hampton University with an advertising and public relations major.

He decided to go to Hampton because of a high school friend. Drew was accepted during his senior year of high school visited in April of that year. He did not have prior knowledge of college life or Hampton specifically. Because of his decision to leave NY and go away to college, his networking in Virginia gave him the opportunity to become the Official DJ for Chris Brown in 2005. He has become a world-renowned traveling DJ. What he gained in college had nothing to do with what he learned in the classroom.

I look at Andrew "DJ Babey Drew" Bisnaught as one of my big brothers and someone I always looked up to, especially when it came to multitasking and getting the job done. The way he multitasked back then was inspiring and his ability to multitask shows during his ventures now. He never used excuses to get out of hard work. He was never "too busy." He is always pushing himself and setting goals. When we were in college, we would plan these extravagant events for Homecoming every year. We would start planning months in advance before school even started. We'd plan five events in three days. We'd sell thousands of tickets…We would market to multiple cities and colleges over a three-month period. I would present ideas to Drew and he would say, "Ok, let's do it." Just like that. It was back then that I began to realize that anything is possible with proper planning and support. You still have to incorporate things you do on a daily basis with future plans and ideas you are turning into a reality. In other words, every single day you should be doing something related to your future goals in life.

The closest relationships I have now started in college. Had it not been for the relationship I started with Drew all the way back in 2001, I wouldn't have met people and created friendships and business relationships with people like Reginald "DJ Regy Reg" Morris current community leader and DJ, Traci Steele, Author, DJ and entrepreneur and Paul Saunders, businessman and entrepreneur just to name a few.

You have to utilize your time wisely to get multiple tasks done. All parts of this book work together to ensure the greatest success. Multi-Tasking is a part of life. Every day you have 24 hours to do various things that make you happy and fill you with pride to have completed.

THIS IS

Being on Time

"To be early is to be on time, to be on time is to be late, and to be late is unacceptable."

I learned this in college early. I set the clock in my car 10 minutes early so I can ensure I get to places early. I got accustomed to getting up 30-40 minutes early in the morning and getting proper rest to function throughout the day.

I'm going to take a time out from teaching about outside the classroom to give a tip that will help get you a higher grade.

Apply this to your everyday life:

- Show up ahead of time.
- When in class sit in the first few seats in the front row
- Always ask three questions a day.

That does a few things:
1. Your professor will always see you in class and on time.
2. It will force you to be attentive.
3. You'll learn more and retain more information.
Something this simple can be the difference between a B and an A.

Take that same approach to being involved in an organization or building a business. When you attend meetings, always arrive early. Pay attention and ask questions. You'll understand the business and you will be better prepared whether it be your own or one you're a part of. No question is a dumb question and chances are someone else in the room is thinking the same thing.

Adjust with the times

No one should ever be unprepared for something unless it is put together at the last minute or something changed dramatically. With the way we can gather information so quickly in today's society, being prepared is one of the easiest things to do that, once again require zero talent. The internet is your best tool. Research topics, take notes, ask questions. For example, if you're on a basketball team, before a big game, you can watch film of the other team and players,

THIS IS WHY

learn their habits and be better prepared to face that opponent. You can prepare in the same way for your success in college.

There was no social media when I started college in 2001. Facebook didn't come around until the middle of college for me And it wasn't the Facebook you know today. You could only be on it if you were a college student and not all colleges were involved. Chris Queen, computer science major and one of my interns, played a big part in getting Facebook to our university.

Now, social media is a major part of everyone's life, especially as a college student. Social media sometimes is viewed as a deterrent to getting work done, a reason for why college students don't socialize the same, and why the morale on campuses isn't the same as it used to be. Nothing is better than in-person social interaction. Nothing will replace that. However, if you look at social media as a tool instead of a barrier, you will be able to use it to your advantage.

If I had social media back when I was in college the way it is available now, I would have been able to reach a much larger audience. You can have an idea and connect with people across the globe with similar ideas. You can find out that no one has a similar idea and that you are on the front end of something new.

Social media now can be used to enhance life, to help you reach the goals you have. Keep in mind you can get addicted to social media just like anything else. If you use social media to your advantage, you will be able to educate yourself by sharing your thoughts with people you don't even now. You can connect with individuals by sending a quick introduction message. I have been able to reach out to people through social media, getting bits and pieces of information for my documentary and this publication.

Because of social media, I have been able to stay in contact with my network whether we live a few miles away or are scattered across the country. With social media, you can promote your brand immediately. Not only can you promote your brand locally, it's going to reach millions of people. Noble causes, fundraisers, service events will be heard and seen by

everyone you reach out to. You can create awareness about an event much easier now. People can comment on your business easier through social media.

THIS IS

You can constantly get new content and people interested in your brand. There are a number of positive ways to use social media. Focus on how it can be useful, rather than on how it can get in the way.

I want you to come up with new innovative ideas! Ask yourself.."What's your Facebook?" I have regretted times when I changed with the time a little later than others. I was late to the party for Twitter, Instagram, and the whole social media wave because I didn't believe in it at the time. I didn't see the point or the reason aside from it being something "fun." Little did I know that Instagram was going to grow to what it is now. Snapchat and LinkedIn were also waves I was late catching onto. I want you to learn from my successes and failures. Always be open to change and adjust when you see the tables turning toward new
technology and communication.

Surround Yourself with Good People

One of my favorite college movies of all time is Higher Learning. In that movie, the character Remy was a quiet freshman from Idaho. From the very beginning of the movie, he was looking for somewhere to fit in. He tried to fit in with this roommates, he even tried to go to fraternity parties. He was looking for acceptance, but it didn't happen. He finally comes across a group of skinheads and dropouts hanging out on campus. They approach him and just like that within a few months he's a full blown Nazi skinhead performing a mass shooting on campus. DON'T BE LIKE REMY! You may think that that is a little extreme, but in all honesty, no one really knows the background as to why things happen and how people meet.

Most people want to have friends and want to feel wanted. Some people may do things to feel needed. Don't follow the wrong crowd just looking for acceptance.

It's very easy, even in college, to get sucked into the wrong crowd. You will find out quickly there are so many different groups of people regardless of the type of school you go to. You want to always surround yourself around positive people who have similar goals.

THIS IS WHY

Merchant's New Face Method for Success
Take Home Notes:

What are your goals? Set up a plan for each goal.
Daily
Weekly
Monthly
Yearly
Set your S. M. A. R. T. Goals
Manage your time
Plan out your day and week
Your day will be a Multi-Task and that is OK
Remember: You have the same 24 hours as Diddy.

For additional assistance on setting goals and planning, contact me by email
Yancy@newfacemanagement.org

resources :
www.cnbc.com
https://www.combsenterprises.com/sean-combs/

THIS IS

Merchant's New Face Method for Success
9 keys to be an Effective College Student outside the classroom

1 -IT'S TIME TO SET YOUR SCHEDULE (DAILY ROUTINE)
2 -Building Character leaders not just successful Leaders
3 - JOIN ORGANIZATIONS
4 - BE THE X FACTOR
5 - BRAND AND INVEST IN YOURSELF
6 - CREATE YOUR N.E.T.W.O.R.K.
7 - DEVELOP YOUR NEW FACE
8 - BE A SERVANT TO THE COMMUNITY
9 - ALWAYS REMEMBER "WE PROMOTE IT"

THIS IS WHY

KEY # 2. PERFECT THINGS THAT REQUIRE ZERO TALENT

Inspirational Person J'vonn Forbes
Building Character leaders not just successful leaders
Intangibles
Don't Quit
References
Takeaways

THIS IS

Inspirational person: J'vonn Forbes

J'vonn Forbes is a West Philadelphia native who graduated from Morehouse College. Employed by Lehman Brothers post-college, J worked on Wall Street for five years. While working at Morgan Stanley in 2008, he started TNE Group with his Morehouse Brother and former Lehman colleague, Omari Palmer. In 2011, J stopped juggling corporate with his entrepreneur endeavors and decided to work full time for himself.

TNE's client list quickly grew to include Billboard, NY Giants, Baltimore Ravens, Issa Rae's Awkward Black Girl and more. TNE became the staple promotional company for young professionals in NYC and produced monthly events attended by an average of 1,000 guests per event. TNE has produced events in Washington, DC, Miami, Atlanta, Vegas and Los Angeles.

In 2014, while managing TNE's success, J began to grow his real estate portfolio. He started by purchasing two properties in West Philadelphia. His first property purchased is still a part of his rental portfolio and his second property was his first rehabbed flip. Since beginning his real estate endeavors, J has successfully rehabbed over 15 properties a year, holding some for his rental portfolio and flipping others.

In 2017, J created his first non-profit, BlackTech Meetup, allowing him to assist his peers, as well as professionals that are a little younger, in obtaining jobs with Fortune 500 companies. BlackTech Meetup has partnered with Facebook, Squarespace, Twitter and more.

J enjoys managing his three companies and spending time with his wife and daughter while residing in the city where he grew up, Philadelphia. He also enjoys traveling, mentoring youth in various communities he's apart of and spending time with his friends.

www.tne-online.com
j@tne-online.com

THIS IS WHY

I FELT THIS SECTION REQUIRED TWO HEADS AS OPPOSED TO ONE.
I ASKED THE FORMER VICE PRESIDENT OF
NEW FACE ENTERTAINMENT, INC. AND COLLEGE GRADUATE,
KARSON AUSTIN, TO CO-WRITE IT WITH ME. THANK YOU VP FOR
ALWAYS BEING THERE HOLDING ME DOWN WHEN I NEED IT!

THIS SECTION IS THE MOST IMPORTANT SECTION OF THE BOOK
BECAUSE IT DEALS WITH THINGS YOU CAN DO THAT REQUIRE NO
TALENT AND NO ONE CAN DICTATE IT BUT YOU. YOU HAVE 100%
CONTROL OVER EVERYTHING IN THIS SECTION. IF YOU KEEP
THESE INTANGIBLES IN MIND DAILY IT WILL PUT YOU FAR AHEAD
OF THE COMPETITION.

THIS IS

Building character leaders not just successful leaders

Based on my method for success, the following terms will be important to learn. Familiarize yourself with them and consider them while going through your daily routine. These are big ideas for you to think about and practice every day. Thinking about these intangibles will open your eyes and put the things you do into a different perspective. As you begin to grow and utilize these skills, you will see a difference in yourself and others around you. Educators call some of these intangible skills you can learn and apply outside the classroom "soft skills" in comparison to courses in college like math, science, economics you learn in the classroom. These are just as important if not more important because you apply them in your everyday life and in the workplace. Being aware of and working on these intangibles will set you up for success and build your character up to be a successful leader. IF YOU KEEP THESE INTANGIBLES IN MIND DAILY, IT WILL PUT YOU FAR AHEAD OF THE COMPETITION.

Victor Rogers graduated from Old Dominion University (ODU) with my internship where he earned a Bachelor of Science degree in Marketing with a minor in Management. During his time at ODU, Victor was the second President of Success Without Limitations (SWL), the student group that I created. When Victor graduated, he expanded the student organization to the campus of Virginia Commonwealth University (VCU) and the campus of Virginia Union University. Vic, like myself, didn't have natural talent. We both had to do a lot to get ahead of those who had gifts and talents that required no learned skill. The word intangible means "something without a physical presence or form," according to Dictionary.com. You can't touch it, but it's there anyway. I use the word "intangibles" to talk about qualities/actions that are very important and require no skill or inherent gifts. In the game of life, every single intangible discussed below can be used every day to put you ahead of the competition in college. The way you approach tasks and obstacles in life is very important. These simple intangibles below can change your life and the lives of the people around you. Plenty of people around the world know these intangibles are needed and tell people they are important; but don't really KNOW how to use them correctly or what they even mean. I will show you now. I want to help build character leaders— not just successful leaders. Being aware of and work-

THIS IS WHY

ing on these intangibles will not only set you up for success but will build your character in a positive direction.

1. Body language

One characteristic you have full control over regardless of talent is body language. Body language is defined as the process of communicating nonverbally through conscious or unconscious gestures and movements. Body language can speak volumes long before the first words are spoken in any situation. Poor body language can derail any interaction regardless of the value you are trying to present verbally. Poor body language is one of my biggest pet peeves and should be yours as well. Facial expressions, posture, fidgetiness are all examples of body language. Whether I'm coaching a game, conducting a meeting, or helping to build a team, body language is the first thing I use to help get my point across. I use my stance, gestures, and eye contact. It can immediately change how a message is being perceived.

Let's say a woman is talking to five friends about a crazy night she had the night before. She's excited to tell her best friends about this night that started off with going out with one of the greatest guys she ever met. But, one girlfriend is not engaged in the conversation; her eyes are not looking in the direction of the speaker. Two other girlfriends have their arms crossed with a "get to the point" look. The other two keep shrugging their shoulders like they could really care less about what she is talking about. How quickly would the woman's excitement dampen until she thinks, "Maybe my night wasn't as good as I thought it was?"

You could tell from the body language of these friends that they weren't really that into the story. Now, take that same example and imagine all five friends are looking directly at the speaker hanging on her every word. Their body language is communicating that they are engaged as she relays every detail of her amazing night. It's the same story, but now she walks away thinking, "It *was* the best night of my life."

We have all been there before. We have all been victims of or witnessed poor body language. I want you to do a stellar job of being mindful of your own body language on a daily basis. If you see the body language of others is causing a negative result in a room, talk to that person in a positive way if it's appropriate to do so. I am quick to tell people to keep their heads up. I would suggest you smile at the person, ask what's wrong, invite them to stand to help ensure they are paying attention. Encourage them not to cross their arms when someone is speaking. How you present yourself affects how you communicate and how positive or negative your experiences will be.

Be mindful of your body language both when presenting information and when receiving it.

Your body language must match what you are trying to convey. When the way you look conflicts with what you are saying, it can be confusing and can send mixed messages to your listener.

Body language includes your entire body. Your eye contact, facial expression, arm placement, hand movements, stance, and posture are always speaking for you especially when you are not speaking aloud. Your body language can be interpreted from a distance, so be mindful of these things at all times.

2.Energy

Energy is defined as a person's physical and mental powers, typically as applied to a particular task or activity. People feel your energy. It's contagious. Have you ever noticed someone can come into the room and change the whole energy of the room whether it be positive or negative? I have always been known as someone that can change a room solely from my energy, no matter if it's five people in the room or five hundred. I take pride in being that person. Be alert and aware of whether or not you are giving off positive or negative energy. Positive energy can open doors to opportunities you didn't even know existed. My goal is to teach you to walk into a room and exude magnetic energy that attracts people.

Remember that negative energy brings attention, too. Sadly, it's not the energy we want to put into existence or surround ourselves with as we are working toward success. I have witnessed it repeatedly; the energy you put into the world is the energy you get back. Think about where your mind is when you are setting goals. Is it in a positive place? Where is the energy when you set these goals? Only you know the answer. I am here to tell you that energy is real.

THIS IS WHY

Energy is a powerful stimulant. Personally, I hate coffee. As a student, I was motivated by throwing parties and making people happy. That gave me the energy I needed like caffeine in coffee. Achieving success and changing people's lives motivated me. I thought I was the local P. Diddy. As I got older, I realized I was good at planning and organizing. I was also good at seeing potential in people and putting them in the right position to be successful. These were my talents. I didn't have them written down on a big vision board, but I had notes I worked on them on a daily basis.

One of the ways you can help yourself stay positive and full of energy is to get proper rest. You have full control over how must rest you get each day. Remember back when I spoke about time management? There are 24 hours in a day. When you are in college – trust me – you will utilize every single one of those hours. Try your best to get six to eight hours of sleep per day. You have to know yourself to know if you can go to sleep at 2am and wake up at 8am every day and function at 110% energy. Are you a night person or a morning person? If you have early classes, will you be sluggish, disengaged, and unfocused? Will you have the right body language, attitude, and work ethic to give your maximum effort? Personally, I have always been a morning person. I like to get my work done as early as possible, whether that be paperwork or working out at the gym. I prefer to do as much as I can before noon so that the rest of the afternoon is left for extra tasks and my personal time. I prefer to be resting by 10pm and asleep by 11pm so that I can be up by 5:30am. I have friends that are just as productive as I am during that same 24 hours who would never get up at 5:30am. They prefer to get up at noon. They get all their work and personal goals completed later in the day or at night while everyone else is asleep. They may go to sleep at 4am then sleep until 11am. Think about your own preferences and rhythms when planning out your daily routine with classes and outside the classroom activities.

Be mindful of what sways your energy. Positive energy can easily be turned into negative energy in certain situations. We all have triggers that can influence our energy either positively or negatively. When you know what alters your energy, you are more aware and can prevent adverse changes that might arise.

Maintaining positive energy is essential throughout your daily process but may not always be easy. Identify things or activities that recharge your positive energy throughout the day when it starts to fade. Things like, music, a good read, a conversation with a friend or loved one, or even just taking a moment to remove yourself from everything going on and spending a few moments by yourself are some examples.

3. Attitude

There was a pivotal moment during a movie called *Remember the Titans* that debuted in 2000 directed by Boaz Yakin starring Denzel Washington and Will Patton. The film was based on a true story that took place in 1971 when two football coaches had to overcome racial segregation. Actor Wood Harris played Julius Campbell, star linebacker. Ryan Hurst played Gerry Bertier, star linebacker and team captain. There was a point in the movie when Julius and Gerry were talking after a bad practice. Julius says, "Attitude reflects leadership, Captain." That was a moment of self-reflection for Gerry; he took a look back at himself and realized that he needed to change his own attitude to influence the attitude of the team. Whether you are in a leadership position or a participant in a larger group, have your attitude be a positive influence on everything you are a part of. The positive and motivational way of thinking changes the perception of the day, event, and situation. The glass is half full, not half empty.

Andrew Bisnaught (DJ Babeydrew) has one of the best attitudes I have ever come across. He has a smile that can light up a room and when he speaks, he immediately comes off as happy and positive. I've known him for almost twenty years and his attitude hasn't changed one bit. I knew him while we were in college and have watched him grow from a radio personality, to a world renowned DJ, to a father, to a multi business owner. He still has the same positive, happy attitude. We have done business together over the years and have had plenty of situations where we expected things to go one way and it went the opposite. We both refused to fail and kept that positive attitude that things would work out in the best way possible. This allowed us to work together and make the impossible possible. Attitude and energy go hand in hand. Very rarely can you say one has good energy but a bad attitude or vice versa.

Being a positive thinker isn't as easy as it sounds for everyone. Our brains are wired to survive, which for some people has meant focusing on negatives in their environment. What I'm saying, though, is that the power of positive

THIS IS WHY

thinking can take you a long way. An example of flipping the script on negative thinking would be looking at a new task and, rather than saying it's too hard, say "it's a fun challenge." Another popular example of positive thinking is how people look at a glass that is filled halfway. Some people say the glass is half-full while others say it's half empty. Who's right? It doesn't really matter. The analogy highlights that some people focus on what they have (it's half-full) and some people focus on what they don't have (it's half-empty). The point is that those people who focus on their strengths and abilities and are able to be grateful for that glass are able to overcome challenges better. I try my best to see the positive in any situation and make the best out of it.

4. Confidence

Confidence is defined as a personal feeling you get when you are free from the uncertainty of your success. You know you will succeed. Confident people have faith in themselves without being arrogant or conceited. This combined with hard work and dedication is one of the most valuable intangibles. Some people are confident but lack the work ethic and dedication to be great though. You still have to work to have something to actually be confident in. People who are confident know that they are able to perform the tasks ahead and it shows in their performance. It's a certain coolness about someone who is confident that it almost makes the other people nearby feel like everything is going to be ok. In order to have that type of confidence, you have to be able to learn and be willing to fail. You have to be open to suggestions and be humble enough to accept help. Having a simple, engaging smile while making eye contact when you walk in, keeping your head up, walking with correct posture are all physical reflections of confidence. You may be feeling shy, but you still need to demand attention. Have that self-assurance that you can get the task done. Wake up every morning and tell yourself, you are great! Tell yourself you will learn something new that will add fuel to your brain. No one knows everything. That's not what it means to be a confident person. A confident person is not a know-it-all. Someone should be confident in their particular skill set. That kind of confidence demands attention.

Booker Forte, a self-taught dancer from Los Angeles, California who now resides in Las Vegas, Nevada is an example of someone who worked hard and has this level of confidence. He started to showcase his talent at an early age and realized that his talent combined with confidence was second to none. He was actually the first dancer to be featured on www.worldstar.com. Once again, he was self-taught but extremely confident in what he had learned and in his skills. He was an America's Got Talent quarter-finalist in 2010, won $10,000 in the George Lopez "Lopez Tonight" "dance done different" contest and was also in a winner in two other TV shows totaling $50,000 in dance contest prizes. He's currently on tour now. Booker was able to build a successful career from teaching himself and having the confidence to take advantage of the opportunities before him.

Confidence in yourself will make others believe in you as well. Being able to speak and present yourself confidently is instrumental in getting buy-in from others. In most cases, when someone has some doubts or questions about what you can offer, your confidence can tip the scale. Be mindful of how you express said confidence. Over confidence and arrogance can lead to negative results. One does not have to be boisterous and loud to be confident. Different situations require different displays of confidence. Being able to identify how to effectively express your confidence in different situations can be a helpful skill in attaining your goals and having support from others in your journey.

5. Be an ACTIVE listener

This seems like the easiest thing, right? Just listen. You have two ears and one mouth for a reason. Listen twice as hard as you speak to respond effectively. Listening is very important in any relationship, no matter the level. It is important to listen to your peers just as much as it's important to listen to your leaders and your mentees. If you take the time to listen to what people are saying without trying to prepare a built-in response based on what you "know" they are going to say, you might be surprised to find that you are a terrible listener. Try this the next time you are at a workshop or having a simple one-on-one conversation. While you are listening, take notes about what is being said.

This is not just actively waiting to talk. Make mental notes of key points you want to share when someone is speaking to you. That way, once you are given a chance to speak, you can respond to the most vital issues being discussed. When others are speaking, try to think about the exact words they are using. If you practice this, you will comprehend and retain a vast majority of the information you hear.

When the speaker is done, repeat in your own words (this is called

THIS IS WHY

paraphrasing) what was said back to the speaker and see how he or she thinks you did. You may think you are listening, but did you hear the message? Did you miss any key points? Learning to listen takes a lot of time and maturity, but it's one of the best skills you can develop. It will help you get through college, personal relationships, and life as a whole. You must hear and pay attention with thoughtful intent.

Try not to listen with intent to speak. Be sure to listen with the intention of gaining understanding of what the other party is saying to you. This will help you develop follow-up questions or may even answer the current questions you have. Understanding what is being said will be instrumental in preparing the next steps of what you are trying to accomplish.

Many underlying messages can be received by active listening. Sometimes things are not said clearly and directly, but if you listen, you can see the direction that the conversation or interaction is headed.

6. Work Ethic

Work ethic is a "belief in the moral benefit and importance of work and its inherent ability to strengthen character." Having a strong work ethic comes naturally to some people. For others it has to be developed and skills have to be applied over time. Remember you're in college for a reason. You need to take advantage of every opportunity given to you. Most opportunities will not be spoon-fed to you. You have to work for things in order to get the most benefit out of them. If you are lazy, the moment will pass and someone else will be there to take what could have been yours.You aren't entitled to anything you didn't work for. Be on top of everything and work hard at it. If you play a sport, step up your game. Be the first and last one on the field and in the gym. If you dance, the same applies in the studio. The support system you are used to at home won't be there, anymore. So if you're used to your mom waking you up early morning for school, you will have to get used to waking up on your own.

I watched the documentary *Can't Stop Won't Stop* more than ten times this year alone. It's a documentary about Bad Boy and Sean "P. Diddy" Combs putting together a reunion concert with all the past members of the Bad Boy Entertainment family. Some of them had not performed or seen each other in decades. While working on the event, director Laurieann Gibson stated,

"Greatness is complicated."

Statements like this resonate with me because they're so true. If you want to be great, there's nothing easy about it. There is no cheat code or easy way to be great. I wish greatness for everyone reading this. But, it's NOT going to be easy. It's going to be very complicated. You have to be willing and able to do things other people are not willing to do. For example, you can't have a goal to be a great performer and not be willing to put in the work needed to become great whether you are performing on the field, on the stage, on the basketball court, in the courtroom or operating room.

Your work ethic should always be at a high level. That comes from within. You have to believe within yourself that what you're trying to accomplish on a daily, monthly, yearly basis is for good. I want you to work hard to obtain your goals. Set your goals and work to obtain those goals. Nothing will be given to you, especially in college.

A strong work ethic is one of the major intangibles that can help you overcome skills and attributes that do not come naturally. You could be the most talented person but easily be outworked and end up losing in the long run. If someone wants it more than you and is willing to put in the work that you are not willing to, the odds of your success are greatly diminished. Never let yourself be outworked by the competition.

When you ask about top performers in anything, the one constant is work ethic. You always want to do things to separate yourself from the competition. Go above and beyond to ensure success. When New Face Entertainment threw parties for college students, we could have just set up a basic DJ event. People would have come and gone having had a fun time. However, we took the opportunity to put on major events – experiences people will remember for life. For example, in 2007, we threw the "best damn party ever" for homecoming. We went above and beyond with our promotions, skipping the usual five thousand flyer distribution, instead putting on a photo shoot with models to create big posters on all the campus stating this event would be "The best damn party ever." We had a total of 20,000 flyers in circulation. We didn't just walk around and talk to people about going to the event...We walked around with blow horns screaming "Best damn party...EVER!" During the event, we didn't just have speakers and a DJ. We had models with fully covered body paint. We had

THIS IS WHY

smoke and lighting. We had giveaways and masquerade masks. We did little, simple things that created a magical experience. People say insanity is doing the same thing over and over and expecting a different result. We knew that homecoming was not just your typical weekend we had to do extra. We had to do something to separate ourselves from the event-planning competition. We didn't want 1,000 people in attendance like usual; we wanted 3,000 people and that's exactly what we got. This is the time to do extra. Make the extra become the norm. Step up expectations and make people realize that you and/or your business are different from the rest.

7. Effort

Some people say effort can't be taught. However, how many times have you heard "he's not even trying" or "she needs to at least try to do it." That's the power of effort. You want to try to utilize your day effectively in high school. You have the same 24 hours, seven days a week as everyone else in the world.

That is the same 24 hours that your friends, enemies, celebrities, and billionaires have. You can put forth the same or more effort to achieve your goals in life by waking up with the intention to attack each day and make it better than the last. Effort is just your attempt to do something, but I want you to look at effort as a gauge to determine how much you put into something. You can put in a little effort or a lot of effort. Let's say you are watching a basketball game. A team is getting blown out by twenty points. If the team gets discouraged and stops playing their best now, they could lose by thirty. If the team gives the game an extra burst of effort and gives the game their all, they could make a comeback and end up winning by ten. This difference in result directly reflects differences in effort by the team. Put forth the effort to be successful. Effort and how much you care about what you're doing go hand and hand. If you genuinely care about what you are trying to accomplish, your effort should reflect that. Distinguish yourself from others in your field by always putting in "maximum effort." Don't ever lose the game of life because you decided not to give enough effort.

Passion is defined as an intense desire or enthusiasm for something.

Care for and take pride in your work. That doesn't just apply to what you do in the classroom, it applies to all areas of your life. You should want success in whatever you're a part of and you should take it personally when it's not. It

THIS IS

should hurt to the core that things didn't go the way initially planned. You should do everything you can to make it better moving forward.

8. Being coachable

Being "coachable" does not only apply to students who are on a sports team. This also applies to those who are a part of ANY team! Being willing to learn is very important. Even if you're the leader of a team, you still have to listen to the other members. You still have to be able to take criticism and interpret it in a positive way, even if it's presented to you in a negative way. If your coach is screaming at you to run a play a particular way, don't put your head down and tuck your tail between your legs. Take it a motivation to get faster and stronger. Keep your head up, consider how to take in the recommendations to get better and maintain a positive way of thinking.

9. Motivation

Motivation means your reason for doing something. Before you take on big projects, ask yourself what drives you to wake up every day and tackle your goals? Every day, I get up with the long-term goal of changing the world. My plan by the time I leave this earth is to leave my mark. That means that I want multiple people to have been positively affected by my actions. That is the number one reason why I wrote this series. I want to inspire people. I want people to read this and change their view on college. I want you to understand that college is not just about going to get the degree. Going to college is more than just sitting in the classroom and learning from a textbook or lecture. That goal is what motivates me right now. My long-term goal is to change the world and one way I am doing that is with the short-term goal of writing this book. I want to put it in the hands of millions of people! I have to get up every day and dedicate time to creating a successful publication for the world to read. What is your motivation? If you have not already done so, consider going back to the access yourself activity in section one. That can give you information about your motivation.

10. Accountability

You are responsible for your actions. Always hold yourself and your peers accountable as well. Accountability is important when you have set goals, especially when you are taking on a new challenge, like college. Again, you no longer have an adult telling you to get up in the morning and go to high school. If you don't get up and take care of business by going to class or an organization meeting, it is 100% on you. It is a great idea to have friends and be accountable to each other. Create a network of like-minded students. It's called having an accountability partner or team. Accountability partners are commonly used for diets or workout plans. You can use accountability partners for anything. It's an easy way to ensure that you and your peers are successful. Some people utilize social media as an accountability partner. Make a post that everyone will see. It can help you feel like now you have no choice but to complete the task, especially if people ask you about it. For example, someone will post "I will lose fifteen pounds in two months." Then, they can post weekly updates on their weight loss journey. Their friends can follow their journey, make comments, give suggestions, and give encouragement. That is a way to use social media as an accountability partner. But first, be accountable for yourself. Really stop and think about what you need to do to be successful. No one knows you like you do. So if, for example, you know you need 30 minutes to get up and get out your apartment or dorm room, you have to be accountable to yourself to know that planning for that 30 minutes is essential. I give myself personal accountability goals all the time. I write them down everywhere. I repeat them to myself and others. I continuously talk about my goals in life and speak them into existence. The reason I do that is to make myself accountable because if I kept it to myself, I would be less likely to get it done.

Keep in mind when dealing with accountability that procrastination can occur. It happens to all of us. You hear or know you have to do something that you have weeks or months to complete. Before you know it, the time is up. Now you are rushing to complete the task and don't give your all because you don't have time. You must be productive everyday throughout your time, especially in college. There is so much "free time" in college, you may feel like there's nothing to do. However, one of the major learning experiences in college is to figure how and when to do things on your own without any "adult" supervision because YOU are an adult now. If you are a part of an organization or get assigned with a task from your peers, no matter how long you think you have to get it done, do it as soon as possible. This extra time allows for any mistakes and ensures that the task is completed well.

11.Having a sense of Urgency

I deal with high school and college students on a consistent basis. I have noticed that the ones who treat tasks they set out to do like checking emails, ideas, plans, work as if it must be done by a certain time or day, they end up more successful overall. Having a relaxed attitude doesn't get things done and by the time it is done too much time has gone by where you could have missed out on other opportunities and/or learned much more. When you have a sense of urgency and avoid as many distractions as possible, that kind of focus on a daily basis will keep you ahead of the competition. That means doing tasks ahead of time. That means caring about your work. That means don't procrastinate.

12.Ask questions

I learned this in college and it has stuck with me to this day. Always ask questions. Ask three questions a day. When you are in class, in a seminar, or learning something new, ask questions. Even if you feel like you know everything, ask questions. Asking a question can go so far and can lead to other ideas and goals. It also shows the people you are with that you are engaged and interested. We always can learn more. Everyone has been a teenager and I know at that age you think adults don't know everything. And it's true, adults don't know it all but neither do teenagers. So there is nothing wrong with asking questions and finding out more information. Ask the same question to multiple people. That may help you feel more comfortable that you are getting the correct information. Feed your brain with as much knowledge as possible.

THIS IS WHY

13. 21/90 rule

I'm a firm believer in the idea that it takes 21 days to make a habit and 90 days to build a lifestyle. If you can commit to 21 days of working hard and actually trying to get better at something, you will be better than you were in the weeks prior. When you take it a step further, it takes 90 days to build a lifestyle. Consistency is the key here. Three months of consistency and building a lifestyle change can go a long way in accomplishing your goals. You cannot continue to do the same thing repeatedly while expecting a different result. The same applies while in college. You change your environment but you also have to change your habits.

Here's a challenge: everyday spend some time practicing looking for the positive in a few challenging situations for 21 days and see if it feels like your ability to see the positive is becoming a habit. The next step, of course, would be to continue to challenge add yourself for 90 days and see how different you look at life.

14. Chivalry and respect

Simple, human decency can go a long way. Smile, say good morning and good afternoon when you see people walk past you. Men, open the door for women. Women, say thank you and smile. Of course, ladies, you can open the door for men, too. We can also smile and say thank you! Remember the golden rule:

Treat others the way you want to be treated yourself.

THIS IS

Don't Quit!

When things go wrong, as they sometimes will,
when the road you're trudging seems all uphill,
When the funds are low and the debts are high,
And you want to smile, but you have to sigh,
When care is pressing you down a bit,
Rest, if you must, but do not quit.
Life is queer with its twists and turns,
As every one of us sometimes learns,
And many a failure turns about,
When he might have won had he stuck it out;
Don't give up though the pace seems slow—
You may succeed with another blow.
Often the goal is nearer than,
It seems to be a faint and faltering man,
Often the struggler has given up,
When he might have captured the victor's cup,
And he learned too late when the night slipped down,
How close he was to the golden crown.
Success is failure turned inside out—
The silver tint of the clouds of doubt,
And you never can tell how close you are,
It may be near when it seems so far,
So stick to the fight when you're hardest hit—
It's when things seem worst that you must not quit.

—Rudyard Kipling

THIS IS WHY

References

https://www.forbes.com/sites/womensmedia/2016/12/21/how-to-train-your-brain-to-go-positive-instead-of-negative/?utm_source=FACEBOOK&utm_medium=social&utm_term=Malorie/#62dd1e035a58

THIS IS

Merchant's New Face Method for Success
Take Home Notes:

UNLIKE OTHER CHAPTERS THESE ARE FOR DAILY USE

Don't just be successful...be a leader
Monitor your body language and the body language of others
Work on your energy
Attitude
Confidence
Be an ACTIVE listener
Work ethic
Effort
Coach and be Coachable
Be accountable
Have a sense of urgency
Ask Questions
21/90 rule
Chivalry & Respect

THIS IS WHY

Merchant's New Face Method for Success
9 keys to be an Effective College Student outside the classroom

1 - IT'S TIME TO SET YOUR SCHEDULE (DAILY ROUTINE)
2 - PERFECT THINGS THAT REQUIRE ZERO TALENT
3 - JOIN ORGANIZATIONS
4 - BE THE X FACTOR
5 - BRAND AND INVEST IN YOURSELF
6 - CREATE YOUR N.E.T.W.O.R.K.
7 - DEVELOP YOUR NEW FACE
8 - BE A SERVANT TO THE COMMUNITY
9 - ALWAYS REMEMBER "WE PROMOTE IT"

THIS IS

V. KEY #3. JOIN ORGANIZATIONS

Featured Organization: Success Without Limitations Old Dominion University
Why should you join a student organization?
Student Union Board
Student Government Associations
Pre alumni associations
Student Leadership Organizations
Fraternities/Sororities
Organizations within your major
ROTC
RA/Dorm Directors
Band and Dance Groups
Sports Teams
The Promoters
Recap
Full Transparency
Checklist
Reading material and websites
References

THIS IS WHY

Featured Organization
Success Without Limitations at Old Dominion University

In 2007, as a graduate student, I, along with undergraduate students on the campus of Old Dominion University created the student organization SWL (Success Without Limitations). The organization is still active with over 200 members. Wakita Taylor, was the first president of SWL and still utilizes what she learned then in her everyday life. After Ms. Taylor, Vic Rogers became the next president and continued to grow the organization expanding it to Richmond, Virginia. The purpose of SWL is to create a culturally-friendly environment through educational, social, and community programming, which will develop leadership and civility among its members. We strive to accomplish our purpose though the co-sponsorship of campus events, extensive community service, family oriented projects, and campus beautification. Success Without Limitations bridges the gap between what is learned in the classroom in college and what is learned outside the classroom such as dealing with anxiety, depression, social gatherings as a young adult and preparing for the conflicts college students may face. Students also have the opportunity to gain internships through the organization strong ties to the community and alumni.

I'm proud that Success Without Limitations is still an active and productive organization on the campus of Old Dominion University. SWLs foundation is built on community service and working with multiple organizations for a common goal. An organization like SWL is great for any student to be involved in. It mentors freshman students; you can join immediately with minimal requirements and as you grow as a college student, it promotes taking leadership positions not only in SWL but in other organizations on campus allowing the networking tree to grow and for organizations to work together creating unity. There are other organizations like this on various campuses, but I have been working diligently to expand Success Without Limitations in high schools and colleges because of what SWL promotes and represents.

The ODU SWL has hosted many events on campus related to education, social, and advocacy goals. One such event was an initiative to bring awareness and support for the water crisis in Flint Michigan. Other events included the 757 DJ Battle featuring the best DJs in the Hampton Roads area and local colleges; a Campus Dating Games; and A Black Art Matters event that featured art talent of students of color.

"Fingers interlocked...not one child left behind"

You can find out more information about Success without Limitations through the ODU organization webpage https://orgsync.com/55777/chapter and on the SWL instagram at www.instagram.com/oduswl

SWL is planning to expand programming to high school and colleges across the country. We want YOU to be a part of the movement.
To learn more about getting involved or starting a SWL chapter at your high school or college, go to www.newfacemanagement.org and click SWL.
Contact SWL via email at Success Without Limitations 2005@gmail.com

THIS IS WHY

Why Should You Join a Student Organization?

Have you ever questioned why you should join a campus organization? Why join a Greek organization? Why be on a sports team knowing you won't be a professional player? Have you consider why you should join the Student Government Association, your local Success Without Limitations chapter, or any other organization?

Joining organizations in college is one of the number one reasons to go to college. Let me tell you why. Getting involved with student organizations can motivate you to push through college when you hit a ditch in your own motivation. There will be times when you start to question your purpose for staying in school to get a degree.

Another reason is that when you join student organizations, you learn how to lead and work with others on a daily basis. You may not have gotten a chance at leadership before, you may even discover a new skill or direction you didn't even know was yours. Being a part of a student group or team gives you a chance to take what you learn in the classroom and immediately to apply that to real life situations. Leadership in student organizations, for example, are the beginnings of learning how to run a business and should be treated as such. Being on time, being accountable, planning, learning, and growing are all a part of successful student participation. This is where you find out what you like and how to learn to work with people, especially when people disagree and have to solve problems together. You get to practice negotiating, plan around events, and weigh out the pros and cons, all while networking with other people. These are invaluable skills and connections that you will use every day after you graduate.

If you go on my website and view the interviews of over 100 college graduates, you will see that over 95% of them agree that they are successful now because they were part of multiple organizations on campus. Through those organizations they built relationships, networked and became the people are today. The decision to join certain organizations, learn, and apply my keys to be successful early in your college career will propel you into being a successful undergrad and alumni. It's easy to go to class, get a degree and graduate but then what? Being a part of organizations on campus is what gets you the experience and puts you in position to have the connections to be successful in your field. My *New Face Method for Success* includes joining organizations that fit your goals and aspirations. Do you remember the Yin Yang reference I made back during the introduction? By being a part of various organizations on your college campus, you learn and grow as a young adult in much different way than from your lectures in the classroom. It is equally important to me.

When I go back to speak on college campuses, I notice how much has changed since I was in graduate school and started SWL in 2007. I noticed that there seems to be a lack of overall student unity I never saw when I was a student. Having active participation in a student organization is one way that you can build a sense of unity, community, and support while you are in school. Unity and support are essential in order to learn and grow and be successful.

Another issue I've seen consistently on college campuses during my visits is that often students do not seem to care about what they are doing. There is often negative competition. Furthermore, many students are joining organizations for the wrong reasons. No one should join an organization for clout or to be popular just to later quit that organization when they become "Greek" or join a more prestigious organization. Coming from someone who held multiple leadership positions, created my own, and took a back seat in others, it doesn't work like that. When you become an upperclassman, you are able to be a part of those more prestigious organizations, you build up those smaller organizations and the people in it because you are LUCKY enough to make it in those more prestigious organizations.

You do not join organizations to create a stepping ladder to get to others. Yes, you join organization to network and meet people who have like-interests. That is great, and I encourage that. But what you don't do is create this ladder for yourself and begin to chop the bottom part of the ladder off as if it didn't exist. The organizations that supported you as an unknown freshman when you didn't have mentors and friends are the ones you need to appreciate. When you become more successful, it is your responsibility to do everything in your power to build them up so they can support other students. I want everyone to keep this in mind when you are on these campuses as students and/or when you

THIS IS WHY

aren't mentoring students. Some of us have the wrong idea of why we join organizations and we have to do better! That is why this section is so important for everyone.

Below are some of the kinds of organizations you may find on campus:

Student Union Board

The University Student Union Board (SUB) is essentially the workhorse of your chosen campus. It's typically one of the easiest organizations you can join. You can join as soon as you enroll on campus and become an active member by going to meetings and joining a committee. I call the SUB the workhorse of the campus because it should have the most members on campus of any other student group. It's usually the group that gets a lot of the legwork done, especially if your campus has an actual student center. It's the responsibility of the SUB to maintain and organize the events for the student body there.

Let's take a look at Ms. Monet N. Clements and her college organization journey. She set foot on her college campus in July of 2000. She eagerly began her journey early by partaking in its per-college program that summer. She wasted no time getting involved in campus life and that summer, she and some of her new friends participated in the talent show hosted by the pre-college students. When freshman year began in September of that same year, Ms. Clements was excited to get back to campus, expand her network, and find out more about student life. Being a competitive cheerleader in High School, she believed that it would be a no brainer to cheer in college. It was quite disappointing to find out that freshmen could not cheer. That motivated her to find out how freshman could get involved. She quickly found herself signing up to be on the Student Union Board (SUB) and trying out for alternate dance team. These were some of the best decisions she could have made because the SUB allowed her to meet many other students and opened the door to many organizations on campus during her tenure.

Ms. Clements danced for one season then tried out for cheerleading and was honored to become a member of Blue Thunder cheerleading squad. In her sophomore year, in addition to being a member of SUB and cheering with Blue Thunder, she became a member of the University Chapter of Habitat for Humanity. In her junior year, Ms. Clements served on the boards for both SUB and Habitat for Humanity. She then had the honor of becoming a member of the Student Leadership Program. Ms. Clements had the pleasure of serving on the SUB all four years and was SUB President her senior year.

Student Government Associations

The Student Government Associations are comprised of students who take concerns to the college administration. They are meant to be a voice of the student body to address any issues to the Deans and President of the University. Student Government Associations, also known as SGA, are also meant to create positions for students to learn and excel where they may have political or advocacy aspirations. The whole student body can participate in SGA, but typically you have to be voted into the leadership positions. It allows students to create campaigns and go out to receive votes as the president, VP, treasurer, secretary, and other organization officers representing your class or other groups.

Shatera Smith, a former SGA member said:

"Even if you do not take a lead position in the student government association, being a member gives you experience working with other students who may or may not be in your major. It also allows you to work on your speaking and negotiation skills."

Shatera is a college graduate with a BA in Political Science, Class of 2005. During her matriculation, she was very involved. She was Ms. Freshman, Vice President of the Class (Sophomore and Junior year), and SGA President (Senior year). She was also a member of several organizations: Student Leaders, Student Recruitment team, and Student Union Board. The University President created an award on her behalf, The Student Leadership Award, because he was amazed by her leadership (she has been the only recipient of the award).

THIS IS WHY

Ms. Smith's advice about life is this:

"God gives you the blueprint of your life; however, it is your responsibility to put it into action. So be wise with the decisions you make because it determines your destiny. Don't regret anything; turn all negatives into a positive and live life to the fullest because tomorrow is not promised."

Pre Alumni Associations

Pre alumni associations give you an opportunity to meet and work with students on campus who are from your home state. The expectation is for you to grow with them during your time in college and upon graduation continue to work together as alumni and build a strong network as professionals.

Sean Washington served as a President of our New York Pre Alumni group, and I served as chair of publicity and marketing during my time at Hampton. Participating in the Pre-Alumni Association gave us the feeling of being at home and allowed us to meet and network with classmates from New York. We took pride in showing others our New York culture, as well, which was fun. As young entrepreneurs, we were able to combine our company with the Pre alumni and host different events. For example, we hosted bodega Fridays in the student center selling chips, juices, and candy as if we were a corner store back home. Students who weren't from New York supported us and had a great time. You can take ideas like that to your pre alumni group and get to experience for yourself.

Student Leadership Organizations

The student leaders are exactly that: the leaders of the students on campus. Student leaders along with Greeks are the "Big Brothers and Big Sisters" on most college campuses. Any type of leadership organization on campus that represents the student body is a great opportunity to learn and mentor.

THIS IS

Here is 2006 Hampton University Business management graduate, Derrick Taylor's take on being a student leader:

"When a freshman comes to Hampton on their first day of new student orientation (NSO) week, their first encounters are typically with the Student Leaders of the campus. These campus peers, students in the Student Leadership Program, welcome you to Hampton University and assist you with not only your indoctrination to the institution, but throughout your entire college journey. Members of the Student Leadership Program inspire and support the student body and faculty through a multitude of student lead activities. The majority of activities at Hampton University are conducted by Student Leaders. At Hampton University, one can study the theoretical application of leadership via the Leadership Institute program, but truly learn how to practically apply leadership as a member of the Student Leadership Program, Because of Yancy, I was inspired to become a Student Leader in order to develop my leadership skills, network campus-wide, and pay it forward to our Home by the Sea community. I'm grateful for my Student Leader experiences, because I'm able to literally leverage them everyday in my church, professional career, and fraternity. Hampton University has a strong alumni network, but this program increases that many times over."

<u>Going Greek (Fraternities/Sororities)</u>

The Fraternities and Sororities on campus are highly respected organizations on campus in one way or another. These are the upperclassmen with Greek letters on their jackets and shirts. They usually walk around campus together and host a number of community service events, seminars, and social gatherings. Becoming a member of a Greek Organization is a different process than joining SUB or SGA. Every organization is different but it typically includes an application and interviews followed by a voting process. You have to at least complete one semester before joining. Some require a year to a year and a half and most have strict Grade Point Average minimums. You can increase your chances of being accepted if you prepare. If you are interested in joining a sorority, for example, research that sorority and that chapter

THIS IS WHY

specifically. Learn the history, know the habits and what they value in prospective pledges. Gather information and prepare yourself in the areas that you have control over. You don't go to class without a pen, right? That's being unprepared.

Greek organizations are national groups, but each school's chapter may be different. The members within the chapters make up the personality of the Greek organization so be mindful of that when making a decision to join one. Also, not every college has the same Greek organizations available to its students. If being a member of a specific Greek organization is important to you whether it be for family legacy or personal aspirations include this in your research when you are considering colleges (See chapter II for other things to consider).

I am a proud brother of Alpha Phi Alpha Fraternity, Incorporated. I was initiated into the Gamma Iota Chapter at Hampton University my sophomore year in college. Although joining any fraternity or sorority has great benefits, I would like to separate The DIVINE 9 from the rest. I made the decision myself to become an Alpha based on what I observed on campus with the various chapters and then did some research. I implore anyone who is interested to do the same.

Charles Stokes, 2004 college graduate, is one of my close friends and has been my fraternity brother for over 15 years. Here is his take on joining college organizations and the Benefit of Leadership and joining organizations.

"I matriculated in Hampton University in the fall of 1999 Majoring in Biology with an Education concentration and immediately immersed myself into campus life and leadership. I ran for Mr. Freshman and won a class a office, became an RA in training for James Hall, was a part of the National Institute of Science club and participated in SGA. Sophomore year I was a full RA in James Hall and then in the new dorm strawberry banks. In the summer of 2000 I joined the US Coast Guard Reserve and became an active reservist AT Station Little Creek located in

Norfolk, VA. Junior year in the fall of 2002 I joined the Student leadership Program, and I pledged the illustrious Gamma Iota Chapter of Alpha Phi Alpha Fraternity Incorporated in the spring of 2002. Senior year

THIS IS

I served on the voting committee, homecoming committee, and spring fest committees respectfully for the student leadership program. In my fraternity, I served as recording secretary for my chapter and liaison to student activities. My second senior year I was elected President of the HU Pan-Hellenic Council, Co-Facilitator to the Student Leadership Program, and Assistant District Director of VACAPAF for Alpha Phi Alpha. These roles proved to be more mentorship roles to members of the organizations and providing servant leadership as well. This was all while maintaining above a 3.0 grade point average. My reasons for joining really boiled down to I felt an opportunity to get out of my comfort zone and expand on my leadership and service capabilities. Being at an HBCU I felt a sense of belonging and community never before felt in High School and I wanted to do my part to make that community strong. Choosing to join these organizations already aligned with my current core values and I saw a positive mutual partnership."

There are nine historically Black Greek letter organizations (BGLOs) that make up the National Pan Hellenic Council. Collectively, these organizations are referred to as "The Divine Nine." Each of these fraternities and sororities is rich in history — ties to one or more of these organizations may be found in many college-educated Black families in the United States.

1. Alpha Phi Alpha Fraternity, Incorporated Founded 1906 on the campus of Cornell University
2. Alpha Kappa Alpha Sorority, Incorporated Founded 1908 on the campus of Howard University
3. Kappa Alpha Psi Fraternity, Incorporated Founded 1911 on the campus of Indiana University
4. Omega Psi Phi Fraternity, Incorporated Founded 1911 on the campus of Howard University
5. Delta Sigma Theta Sorority, Incorporated Founded 1913 on the campus of Howard University
6. Phi Beta Sigma Fraternity, Incorporated Founded 1914 on the campus of Howard University
7. Zeta Phi Beta Sorority, Incorporated Founded 1920 on the campus of Howard University
8. Sigma Gamma Rho Sorority, Incorporated Founded 1922 on the campus of Butler University

THIS IS WHY

9. Iota Phi Theta Fraternity, Incorporated Founded 1963 on the campus of
Morgan State University

Organizations within your major

There are organizations specific to your actual major that will help you be successful outside the classroom. Bianca Cannon was a freshman at Hampton University in the fall of 2003. She is from Long Island, New York and actually went to High School with me and Sean. We had no idea she was coming to Hampton, but it was a pleasant surprise to have another member of the Hills West family down in Virginia with us. Bianca graduated with a degree in nursing, was a part of New Face Entertainment, and participated in the Terpsichorean dance company on campus. She is also a sister of Chi Eta Phi Sorority, Incorporated.

"Chi Eta Phi Sorority is a professional organization of registered nurses and nursing students. Aliene C. Ewell, RN organized the Sorority on October 16, 1932 with the assistance of 11 other courageous registered nurses. The charter chapter, Alpha, was organized at Freedman's Hospital in Washington D.C. for two specific purposes: (1) elevating the plane of nursing and (2) increasing interest in the field of nursing. The graduate and undergraduate (Beta) chapters are grouped into five regions according to geographic areas. The chapters are located throughout the United States, District of Columbia and St. Thomas, US Virgin Island. Chi Eta Phi Sorority, Incorporated is a professional organization for registered professional nurses and student nurses (male and female) representing many cultures and diverse ethnic backgrounds. More than 8000 Registered Nurses and Student Nurses hold membership in Chi Eta Phi Sorority, Incorporated. There are over 101 graduate chapters and 41 undergraduate chapters located in 33 states, District of Columbia and St. Thomas, US Virgin Islands. Membership is by invitation and is both active and honorary. The mission of Chi Eta phi Sorority, Inc. is to

encourage the pursuit of continued education , recruitment programs for health careers, stimulation of close friendly relationships among members, development of working relationships with other professional groups and identification of core nursing leaders who affect social changes at a national regional and local level .Guided by the motto "Service for Humanity", the Sorority has Programs focusing on health promotion/disease prevention, leadership development, mentoring,

THIS IS

recruitment, retention and scholarship."

For more information on Chi Eta Phi, sorority Inc. you can visit its website www.chietaphi.com

Bianca's involvement with Chi Eta Phi in conjunction with her degree set her up for success. Had she just stayed in class and graduated without being active outside the classroom, her journey to advance in her career would have been much harder.

These organizations/teams are important as they can be options related to financial planning and graduating from college with minimal to no debt.

ROTC

ROTC stands for Reserve Officers' Training Corps. ROTC programs train college students to become commissioned officers in the US armed forces while in college. It's another option for financial assistance, future employment serving your country, and connecting with other students who share military interests. I personally wasn't in the ROTC but I have a close friend who was. William Hicks, CPT shared his experiences from ROTC in both college and high school.

"ROTC just like the Army taught me management and leadership skills. Which is why when I threw parties. I understood the project management strategy which in the Army we call it the 5 paragraph operations order. It is the foundation and planning tool used to plan any major event or project. I was already enlisted in the Army so I was receiving funding from simultaneous membership program through the military. I applied for HU when I was deployed in Afghanistan and was accepted before I returned gone from country. I joined the Army in the 11th grade. I had to drill one weekend a month in the Army Reserves which included a monthly salary and 2 weeks 1 time a year on active duty. I received $4,500 a year for classes, HU ROTC covered my room and board and I received a $350-$400 monthly stipend. I was also receiving GI Bill stipend of roughly $800-$1,100 a month for the time I spent in

THIS IS WHY

*Afghanistan and becoming a veteran. I also had a part-time job and I
threw parties on the side when given the opportunity around my class
schedule and army ROTC schedule. I was eligible for loans, and I received a Pell grant. Most of my refund checks I used to invest in
Sneakerboy Entertainment to throw parties. I didn't waste it all on
clothes and shoes like the normal young college student."*

Residence assistant/Dorm directors

A resident assistant (RA) is a great way to not only learn how to manage
people but a way to meet students constantly and learn responsibility. The job
of an RA is to live in a residence hall or dorm and focus on enhancing the
quality of life in the residence halls, including fostering community, providing
academic support, and being attentive to safety and security of residents. The
position requires an individual who is flexible enough to assume a variety of
roles as dictated by the changing needs of students. It is crucial that an
individual be able to relate well to others and handle administrative
responsibilities. The RA is not just an upperclassmen friend in the dorms. They
are the crucial link in creating an environment in which students develop
independence and learn to live cooperatively with others. The job of a dorm
director is to be in charge of RAs. Being an RA is also a way to help pay for
your college education as some positions pay for portions of your tuition
and/or fees. As a dorm director, you are in charge of not only the Ras, but the
whole dorm, its residents, and the building.

Dance Organizations

The Terpsichorean Dance Company is a dance company that incorporates
many styles (e.g., ballet, tap, African, hip hop) of dance at Hampton University.
They practice and perform year round for their own performances and for
organizational events. They do guest performances for pageants, as well.
Dance companies vary on across college campuses and some even offer
scholarships. Cheerleaders like Monet are available on most campuses as well.
Then you have dancers that aren't cheerleaders or a part of a dance company
like "Terps," you have a more modern/recreational group of dancers. On my
campus, they called themselves The Majestic. They performed at halftime of
basketball games and performed at various events. When I was in college, there
were no males in The Majestic but there were males who were extremely

THIS IS

talented and wanted to join. That was an opportunity to create a group for male dancers, hence the birth of The Oracle.

I have close friends within my network who were not only on dance teams in college but created their own leaving a legacy in the music and dance as a part of the Majestic, Oracle, and Terpsichorean Dance Company. Karson Austin, Sean "Fresh" Redding, Tyrell Clay, Crystal Neal, Chris Cardwell, Rob Rich, Day'nah Cooper, Booker Forte, and Kiira Harper are all friends of mine who were ahead of their time. They are now are famous in their respective crafts Karson Austin is mentoring by teaching choreography to college dancers. Crystal Neal is the creative director of the Terpsichorean Dance Company. Chris Cardwell went from being a performer to owning his own photography company booking for professional athletes and companies. Kiira, Rob, Day'-nah Fresh, and Booker have won various awards, toured and performed on stage with artists such as Kendrick Lamar, Beyonce, Ciara, appeared on award shows, received awards, along with owning their own businesses. They were some of the most talented people I ever met. As their peers, I looked up to each one of them for their natural talents in dance and being able to perform at a moment's notice.

If you want to hear more about the story of The Oracle can be seen on the documentary on www.thisiswhydoc.com

THE BAND

I was not a member of the band but an intern of mine, Dominique Wilkins, was kind enough to speak on her experience as a member of the band:

> "Being a diligent musician unlocked many doors, including academic ones, for me as a student. Because I worked really hard at my craft, I was able to audition for Mr. Barney Smart (former Hampton University Director of Bands) and in addition to a band scholarship, he secured a Full Presidential Scholarship for me."

Even if you are not on scholarship like Dominique being a part of the band. If you play an instrument and love music. Being a part of the band is a great way to meet people and when you have that home sick feeling, something like the Band family and bond will keep you going. According to scholarships.com students to complete band courses do better academically compared to those who don't.

THIS IS WHY

Be sure to do your due diligence to see what universities fit your goals and offer scholarships in this field.

Sports Team

Being on a sports team in college is said to be the easiest way to transition from high school to college. Partly this is because even before freshman year starts, you are introduced to members of your team as early as your senior year in high school. You immediately have people with commonalities in an unknown environment. That helps you feel comfortable in an uncomfortable environment. I mentioned in the first chapter starting in High school you can utilize sports to completely pay for your college education. It takes a lot of hard work and dedication at an early age and support at that age has to come family and that initial network I referred to earlier. So playing on a sports team can help pay for your education and help you create an instant network in your sports family. You will learn with these friends and grow with them throughout college and beyond.

Bruce Brown is one of my close friends. I met him at Hampton University as a manager of the basketball team during my freshman year. I was given the task of keeping this seven-foot tall freshman focused in school and in the gym because he was ineligible to play his first year. It was one of the best opportunities I was given within a month of being on campus. Bruce reminded me of Shaquille O'Neal, NBA champion with the LA Lakers and the Miami Heat. Bruce would dance, sing, and talk to everyone who would listen. He is one of the most kind-hearted people you will ever meet. Of course, his height commands instant attention. I used to be hard on him because I knew the potential he had if he would stay focused and work on his craft of basketball. He had a full scholarship to play for the school. Our team had just won the Mid-Eastern Athletic Conference 2000-2001 championship and had upset Ohio State in the NCAA tournament the year before so our name was on the map. We held on to the championship the next year 2001-2002 and became back-to-back champions.

The Promoters

Being a promoter isn't an official student organization on campus but they are a part of every college. What's a college campus without parties? No matter what college you go to, there will be parties the first night you get there and ongoing far past your graduation. No matter the theme, no matter the reason, there are always party promoters who make sure you know which are the best parties to go to every week. If not for the promoters, there would be no party, no fun, and no way to know how to enjoy life on or off campus. Usually, the most popular people on campus tell everyone what party they will be at and the crowd follows. Some party promoters play sports, some are Greek, some are just promoters. Nonetheless, they are the heartbeat of off-campus partying. You may become a promoter. You may be the one who goes to the promoter to find out where to get a ticket or directions.

Being a promoter on campus builds your popularity fast. It is also a way to meet new people and forces you to network and talk to people. Having to persuade people to go to various events every week is not an easy task. Even with social media today, you have to persuade people to go out and spend their money in exchange for a good time.

One additional perk of being a promoter compared to joining other organizations is that you have an opportunity to make money and anytime you are making money, you are also learning how to run a business.

"I look at a college as a playground to the real world. Going into college, I knew this was my first real chance in learning how to be an adult and how the world works in a microcosm. A mentor of mine (Brand With Drew) told me on the first day I stepped foot on the campus of Hampton University, that it was key to network and get involved in as many worthwhile and beneficial organizations/groups as possible while simultaneously putting my true talents and passions to the test, in which I did. The first thing I did was brand myself as "Tray-Kash." It was a combination of my old DJ name from back home (DJ KASH) and my twitter handle I was known by on the first week of school (@Tra_OlCOolAss). So who was this kid? What was his brand? THE CAMPUS HOST, the person where all things entertainment were filtered through. I had the talent, and the name but didn't have the platform or the proper network, so I joined the Greer Dawson Wilson Student Leadership and Training Program on campus (SLP). SLP gave me a platform like no other, allowing me to host/promote official campus events, being the first person you witness on the stage during new student orientation week, and even being the face of recruitment (with the help of the office of admissions). Through SLP I was able to not only host events, concerts, meet major A-

THIS IS WHY

List entertainers and greet them accordingly, it also gave me the oppor-
tunity to understand structure/logistics and what it takes to successfully
curate a super dope experience for the students, for the culture. By the
time my senior year rolled around, I accomplished the unimaginable at
small university in a small harbor town in southern Virginia. A valuable
lesson I learned through my own experiences is that barriers don't exist.
My tenure was filled with kicking down doors and creating my own lane.
I am now applying these ideas and concepts to the macrocosm! One day
I aspire to walk amongst legends like Barry Gordy, Quincy Jones, Sean
Combs, and Shawn Carter."

- Tra'Von "TrayKash" Williams

Hampton University c/o 2016

I want to give a personal reflection of how quickly being a part of
organizations and networking within them can open doors.

"When I received my MEAC champion ring as a manager in 2002. I was
hyped and humble at the same time. Bruce Brown, my close friend who I
was training our freshman year, went on to win another MEAC champi-
onship for Hampton University in the 2005-2006 year while I looked on
as a promoter for the MEAC championship in Raleigh, North Carolina .
He received all MEAC first team honors in 2005 along with MEAC all
tournament team both in 2005 and 2006. It was one of the greatest

feelings to see one of my best friends achieve the goal we set out our
freshman year and because of everything I worked on as a company I
was able to bring down a team of interns from my company to support
Bruce and the team. Rooms were paid for the week, we enjoyed parties,
etc. We were honored to be hired to promote the MEAC in

North Carolina. Afterwards, I was hired to be step show judge because of
my background as a brother of Alpha Phi Alpha Fraternity, Inc. "

If you notice how it can all come together when you network and maintain
relationships.

THIS IS

<u>RECAP</u>

Being a part of any organization on a college campus is your first glimpse of what's it's like working for a company. If you look at it like that, when it comes time for you to be a part of a company or own your own business, it will be like second-nature to you. You won't go in not knowing about how to plan meetings, understand company structure, build a network, or organize events. That is the purpose of joining organizations…the yin to the classroom yang.

Joining an organization can also provide you with people who will become your new extended family. You never know whom you will meet and how they will affect your life in the future.

As we move on from the organization section, I want to point out that it is acceptable to reject an organization that isn't a good fit for you. Do your due diligence ahead of time to find out what groups are available. It may be the time to start your own organization on campus. I saw a need for Success Without Limitations and students expressed interest in it. I encourage you all to seek out like-minded people and organizations where you can make a difference in the community. If you don't find any, that means you need to start your own. What is unethical is to join organizations, take leadership positions, and leave it after you found something better.

The underlying sentiment is to go out and meet new people. Talk to people, meet new friends, and socialize. Look at the upperclassmen on campus. There may be one who you as an inspiration for your future self.

Go to organizational fair. An organization fair on campus is where all student organizations display information and give you an opportunity to find out basic information of all campus organizations. It usually takes place once each semester.

Once you join an organization, you choose to be a part of, consider becoming a leader within those organizations. Don't just join and be a member. Join and take on leadership positions. Get the experience of leading your peers, speaking in public, and organizing events. Become leaders in the organization similar to your goals in life. That is, if you want to be a writer or journalist, for

THIS IS WHY

example, run for secretary of your student group. If you want to learn about money management, run for treasurer. If you want to be an entrepreneur/businessman, run for the position of president or vice-president.

Teaching your peers is important in the learning process. If you can lead people who are your age and education level, it will be much easier to lead people who look up to you. All the people mentioned in this section were leaders of organizations, mentoring peers, and helping them rise to leadership positions.

THIS IS

For full transparency, here is a list of student organizations I was a part or created while in college:

<u>Organizational Resume</u>
James Yancy Merchant, Jr.

Freshman year 2001-2002 Created own event planning company Straight Face/New York Pre-Alumni Member, Publicity Co-Chair, student Union board member, Hampton University Basketball Manager/Trainer
Sophomore year 2002-2003 owner of Straight Face Entertainment New York pre alumni member recording secretary/publicity advisor, Student Union Board member, Student Government Association member: women's caucus, Student Leadership Program member, promotions and marketing co-chair, bazaar co chair, intake committee, community service committee
Spring 2003 initiate into the Gamma Iota Chapter of Alpha Phi Alpha Fraternity, Inc, bigger circle museum organization member publicity advisor, national Pan Hellenic council member promotion and marketing chair
Junior year 2003-2004 owner of now New Face Entertainment created 12-2 in the student center , New York pre alumni recording secretary, Student Union board member, Student Government Association member: women's caucus, Student Leadership Program : promotions and marketing committee, bazaar chair , intake committee , special events committee, Alpha Phi Alpha Fraternity, Inc. Gamma Iota Vice President, National pan Hellenic council member: promotions and marketing chair
Senior year 2004-2005 Owner of New Face Entertainment, LLC , created community service organization Success Without Limitations, New York pre alumni member, SGA member: senate, SLP co facilitator bazaar committee, promotions and marketing, special events committee, spirit committee, intake committee Alpha Phi Alpha fraternity, Inc. Gamma Iota president and financial secretary, National Pan Hellenic council member, promotions and marketing chair.
Graduate Student 2006-2007 at Old Dominion University
Brother of the graduate chapter of Delta Beta Lambda of Alpha Phi Alpha Fraternity, Inc Owner of New Face Entertainment,Inc. started the student organization Success Without Limitations on the campus of ODU.

THIS IS WHY

Merchant's New Face Method for Success
Take Home Notes:

Do your research

Go to the organizational Fair on Campus
Join Organizations
Look for a mentor then become a mentee when you are ready

Join organizations and lead within
Look to work with like organizations
Treat your organizations like a real job, learn and climb the ladder

Reading material and websites

The divine 9 by Lawrence Ross

(Article on top Greeks for various categories)

https://www.townandcountrymag.com/leisure/g10351016/best-fraternities/

References

www.thisiswhydoc.com

www.chietaphi.com

https://www.goarmy.com/rotc.html

The ONE thing by Gary Zeller

THIS IS WHY

Merchant's New Face Method for Success
9 keys to be an Effective College Student outside the classroom

1 - IT'S TIME TO SET YOUR SCHEDULE (DAILY ROUTINE)
2 - PERFECT THINGS THAT REQUIRE ZERO TALENT IT'S TIME TO
SET YOUR SCHEDULE
3 - JOIN ORGANIZATIONS
4 - BE THE X FACTOR
5 - BRAND AND INVEST IN YOURSELF
6 - CREATE YOUR N.E.T.W.O.R.K.
7 - DEVELOP YOUR NEW FACE
8 - BE A SERVANT TO THE COMMUNITY
9 - ALWAYS REMEMBER "WE PROMOTE IT"

THIS IS

KEY #4. BE THE X FACTOR

Taylor James
Kiira Harper
Risk Poem
Find a need/Fulfill the Need
Believe
Invest in Yourself
Branding
Overcome Fear
Motivational Quotes
References
Take Home Notes

THIS IS WHY

People of inspiration
Taylor James

DJ Tay James has been making a name for himself behind the turntables and on the microphone since the age of 16. In 2009, however, just months after graduating from Hampton University in 2009 where he'd made a name for himself as the most-in-demand DJ in the mid-Atlantic, Justin Bieber hired James to join his live show as the tour DJ. Since then, James continues to travel the world performing alongside Bieber and introducing his talent to sold-out crowds around the globe at radio shows, stadium concerts, and festivals.

When he's not on the road with the pop sensation, James continues to headline nightclubs around the world, including his residencies at Playhouse (Los Angeles), FLUXX (San Diego), Muzik (Toronto), and Prive (Atlanta). He is also called upon by an extensive list of celebrity and corporate clients, such as Russell Simmons, Chris Brown, Fabolous, Bow Wow, Beats by Dre, and Adidas, to deejay their private events.

James has performed on some of the highest rated television shows such as The Oprah Winfrey Show, The Ellen Degeneres Show, Jay Leno, the Tonight Show with David Letterman, and NBC's The Today Show. He's also been featured in publications including Teen Vogue, Vibe, Hollywood Life, The Washington Post, Global Grind, and Earmilk.

www.instagram.com/djtayjames
www. djtayjames.com
#weknowthedj

THIS IS

Kiira Harper

Kiira Harper, from Long Island, NY; started her dance journey at the age of seven. Training in various styles, (tap, jazz, ballet, hip-hop, modern, contemporary and African) Kiira learned from an early age how important it was to be a well-rounded individual.

After graduating high school, she attended Hampton University with a minor in Public Relations, and participating in the Terpsichorean Dance Company for all four years. Her professional career began in 2011, and has since then taken off. Her career has been blessed by Beyonce, Trey Songz, Alicia Keys, Jidenna, Tank, Camilla Cabello, and many more.

She now continues her career living in Los Angeles California, while teaching Commercial Heels Classes "Simply stiletto by Kiira Harper" to students all around the country, and internationally. Her heels style is a mix of a deep hip-hop pocket, feminine movement, and jazz technique.

Each class is different, challenging students to pull from within and trust their bodies. Kiira makes sure to use her platform for good, inspiring the women and men that she comes in contact with to fight for change, acceptance, and to never give up on their dreams.

www.instragram.com/kiiraharper
http://cleartalentgroup.com/client/kiira-harper-educator/

Risk Poem

To laugh is to risk appearing the fool.
To weep is to risk appearing sentimental.
To reach out to another is to risk involvement.
To expose feelings is to risk exposing your true self.
To place your dreams, ideas before a crowd is to risk their loss.
To love is to risk not being loved in return.
To live is to risk dying. To hope is to risk despair.
To try is to risk failure.

But to risk we must, because the greatest hazard in life is to risk nothing at all.

The person who risks nothing, does nothing, has nothing, and is nothing.

-Author Unknown

"The greatest successes come from having the freedom to fail."

Mark Zuckerberg

THIS IS

FIND A NEED FULFILL THAT NEED

Anyone who goes to college can find their niche one way or another. Look around. There is always a need that YOU can fill. When Sean and I were college freshman, we saw there was a need for the freshman to enjoy themselves within the guidelines of curfew.
YES WE HAD CURFEW THE FIRST SEMESTER!
We wanted to have fun and had the advantage of my cousin living off campus within walking distance from school. Being best friends, from New York with outgoing personalities led to us becoming popular within the first few days of school. We threw our first house party within two weeks of school starting with one flyer.

The flyer was a simple 8-1/2 by 11 piece of paper that stated

Come party this Friday at the

4th red door on the right over the bridge

with Sean, Yancy, and Howard

Little did we know, that was the beginning of something bigger. We went from throwing house parties to hosting sold out events with thousands of people every week. It's up to you to find as needed. The need can be anything that will allow you to make a difference on your college experience and the experience of others.

Taylor James saw a need to bring exclusive deejaying and a different type of music to his University. He was a freshman business management major at Hampton University in 2005. From Baltimore, Maryland, this young DJ was somehow cocky and humble at the same time. He deserved to be. Now known internationally as DJ Tay James, Official DJ to Justin Bieber, back in 2005 Tay was just my little brother. He was someone just looking for his opportunity to become a legacy. He hit the campus running, giving our over 1,000 copies of his first mixtape. I was always hard on Tay because everyone loved him and I wanted to make sure he remained humble and grateful for the opportunities he had. Earlier that year, I had taken over the reigns of the entertainment crew

THIS IS WHY

Sean, Howard and I had going and turned it into an actual company: New Face Entertainment, Incorporated. When I met Tay, he was looking for opportunities to DJ events and I was looking to expand the company. It was perfect. He was able to go to school and work for New Face doing what he loved. Because of his hard work on his craft, I gave him a raise his sophomore year, and he earned a scholarship through the company. He was able to pay his initiation fee to become an initiate of the Gamma Iota Chapter brother of Alpha Phi Alpha, Fraternity, Inc. Taylor now is my fraternity brother and paving his own way in life. His slogan "We know the DJ" took the campus and various cities up the East coast by storm. He began to use his connections back in the DC area to be on the radio and DJ the biggest clubs at the time in DC. He is a perfect example of not waiting to change the world. Change it now. I saw a need on campus and filled it. He and his business partners at the time had students traveling every week to make money doing what they love from The Hampton roads area to DC and coming back for class. Tay was pivotal in the expansion of New Face, especially with the mixtapes we released every semester. In 2007, there was Facebook, but it wasn't the platform we have today. We were out passing out CDs and promotional material seven days a week. We were all college students working and building our brands.

Believe in yourself

I am a big believer in speaking things into existence. I love to visualize what I want to do and see myself executing whatever it is. I would even plan what to do if it were to go wrong and how I could adjust it. The Secret by Rhonda Byrne talks about the laws of attraction and speaking into existence. I was always confident because I do not allow myself to believe anything less. You have to be your own number one fan. No one knows you better than you. You can create your best self and you have an obligation to do so. We are all here to make a difference in this world. Your biggest competition is always you. Self-confidence is defined as showing poise and confidence in your own worth. No one should have to tell you you're great. You should know you are and prove it in what you do. Strive to be better than the best no matter what.

Kiira Harper is one of the People of Inspiration for this chapter because she felt that my company and I helped her feel at home in college. As you can see, she is also an inspiration for all. She is a dancer and businesswoman with the type of confidence and fearlessness that I would only hope to have a glimpse of. The way she performed on the stage in college was breathtaking. She was a master of every style of dance. Not only were her performances on stage worth mentioning, the way she carried herself with such confidence, you would never know that she thinks of herself as the shy person she claims to be in her interview.

Ms. Harper has made Super Bowl appearances and performed with Beyonce at Coachella. She runs her company "Simply Stiletto" across the world. It is amazing, but I knew the minute I saw her that she was something special. When I hosted an in-the-industry panel, her college dance company, the Terpsichorean Dance Company, co-hosted. The look that these young dancers had on their faces meeting her for the first time was breathtaking. Kiira has become a legacy. She's so humble about her accomplishments, she doesn't even know what a Phenom she is.

Get Hungry

I always knew I had a talent that can bring the best out of people. I'm a motivator; I can sell water to a whale. I see potential in people before they do. Mark Jackson is one of my close friends. I used to call him Jamie Foxx in college because he's so talented in so many things it was like whatever he decided to do I knew he would be great at it. I could see him being an actor, comedian, writer, or musician just like Jamie Foxx. We hosted various events together as undergraduate students such as a "you got served" competition in the campus student center. We also did business together with my company where we conducted fundraiser events to raise money for his chapter of Omega Psi Phi Fraternity, Inc. Mark taught me to be fearless. If you want to do something, do it.

Blake Kelly is another example of someone I saw potential in and stayed on him about being successful. I always tried to make everyone who worked for me as happy and comfortable as possible. When I was in graduate school and looking to take on more of a manager role without Sean by my side, I decided to give others the opportunity to be in the spotlight. Being that Blake and Tay were close friends, I began to push the envelope of Blake being on the mic as the hype man for events that Tay deejayed. I really didn't know that Blake had musical aspirations until he released a track with another friend of mine, Jo Stunnah. But that's how things happen. Blake and Jo went on to become rap artists releasing multiple albums and performing across the world. They have always been hungry and invested in themselves to be successful. They had the

THIS IS WHY

fearlessness I didn't have. They were willing to take certain risks during those prime years I maybe should have done. Those risks paid off for them, but that wasn't without hard with and dedication. Nothing is easy and nothing comes without a struggle.

"Without struggle there is no progress"-Frederick Douglass

These are your prime years of development. You have to make sure you invest in yourself. You have to learn and grow. Use these stories to inspire you and your peers. Anything is possible. Take risks. Continue to be motivated throughout your life and never stop hustling to achieve your goals.

THIS IS

<u>Overcoming fear/taking risk</u>

I take a "hands on" approach to everything. There's only so much you can learn in a classroom the information needs to be applied. You can plan all day but if you don't physically do what you're planning, the plan is worthless. The objective in college is to LEARN and you can learn more outside of the classroom than inside while in college.

You have to take risks in order to be successful. Now, in my mid thirties, I think about risk versus reward often. When I was in my twenties, I wasn't concerned about it at all.

Day'Nah Cooper took the ultimate risk. I will never forget it because I had the opportunity to take the same risk and wasn't as strong as she and the rest of my peers were. It was the spring of 2008 and a group of my friends decided to drive to California in hopes of "making it." Day'Nah had a natural talent to dance and sing. Most of my friends, including now world known choreographers Rob Rich and Sean "Fresh" Redding, had the type of passion and talent in dance, I felt like I didn't have " it" as a manager at the time. I didn't believe in myself and didn't feel comfortable taking that type of risk to leave everything and go to California.

My advice right now is you have to know it's ok to fail. Test your limits some-times you have to get uncomfortable to get there. There are two points in my life where I know now that if I made a decision to take a risk, my future would have ended up much different. Who knows how my story would be at this point but I do know I think about that decision to go to California to this day but everything happens for a reason.

THIS IS WHY

Motivational Quotes

Carpe Diem- Seize the day

There are 7 days in the week. "Someday" isn't one of them.

"It's supposed to be hard. If it wasn't hard, everyone would do it. The hard is what makes it great."--Tom Hanks, "A League of Their Own"

"My life don't work like that... I can make anything happen."-Sean Combs, Can't Stop Won't Stop Documentary

"Learn by doing not by theory." - Chandler Bolt Author of Published

References

The Secret by Rhonda Byrne

THIS IS

Merchant's New Face Method for Success
Take Home Notes:

What is your X-Factor ?

Find the Need and fulfill it?

What separates you from the rest?

Believe and invest in yourself.

THIS IS WHY

Merchant's New Face Method for Success
9 keys to be an Effective College Student outside the classroom

1 - IT'S TIME TO SET YOUR SCHEDULE (DAILY ROUTINE)
2 - PERFECT THINGS THAT REQUIRE ZERO TALENT IT'S TIME TO
SET YOUR SCHEDULE
3 - JOIN ORGANIZATIONS
4 - BE THE X FACTOR
5 - BRAND AND INVEST IN YOURSELF
6 - CREATE YOUR N.E.T.W.O.R.K.
7 - DEVELOP YOUR NEW FACE
8 - BE A SERVANT TO THE COMMUNITY
9 - ALWAYS REMEMBER "WE PROMOTE IT"

THIS IS

KEY# 5.BRAND AND INVEST IN YOURSELF
Anika Williams
What do you want?
Eight steps
Business Cards
Resume
Cover letter
Internships
Create something
12-2
Business Plan
Financial literacy and Management
Tatiani Favors Advice

THIS IS WHY

Person of Inspiration

<u>Anika Williams</u>

Anika is a recent Graduate of Old Dominion University with a major in Communications and a double minor in Marketing and Film and currently attends ODU as a Graduate student in the Humanities Program. She works tremendously hard as a leader and a creative in a multitude of rewarding ways. She is the current president of SWL and the Public Relations Chair for the ODU Chapter of the NAACP. Additionally, serves as a Resident Assistant on campus providing programming, acting as a resource for students and engaging in crisis management. She has a passion for people and work to bring awareness of issues plaguing our community, provide opportunities for creatives in the area to promote themselves and thrive and to bring positivity to the community.

Anika is the PROUD founder and CEO of 3 businesses: NOISIA a clothing brand, Flourished homemade skin care brand and Lemonade Lab a naturally delicious lemonade brand. She has a passion for everything she does including idea development, event planning and working with and for the community.

NOISIA is a clothing brand whose mission is to inspire others to make their vision become a reality, community engagement and uplifting along with supporting the arts and the creatives who provide them. This brand partners with ODU and the surrounding community to provide events that bring attention to the arts and creatives in the area. This brand also focuses on providing outreach and support to children and promote positive thinking and planning for the future.

"Your perception is your reality."

THIS IS

What do you want?

At some point, you have to figure out what you want in life. What are your goals? How you do you want to be successful. What do you want to be known you for? What do you want your legacy to be? Now, some people don't know what they want entering college. It may be easier to just think about abstract ideas at first, or to consider what you *don't want* for your future. Maybe you have an idea of what makes you happy. Once you decide to do things that make you happy, no matter what it is, it's like you can work without feeling like you're working. There's an old saying. "Do what you love and you will never work a day in your life." So, what do you love?

You need to be your own number one fan. As a fan, you have to invest in yourself and create a brand for who you are and what you are here for. I feel everyone was put on this world to change it in some way. Every person plays a role in shaping their own lives and the lives of others. I tell myself daily that I am here to change the world. How I want to change the world has been pretty consistent. I may have had to make a couple turns or some delays in achieving that goal but I'm always headed in the same direction. I know I have always wanted to change the world by leaving a lasting impression on youth that come after me. When I was in college, I wanted to start an after school program for academics and sports for high schoolers. I haven't gotten to that goal, yet, but along the way I have made different strides toward achieving the goal of changing as many lives in our youth as possible.

<u>Create your Brand</u>

Being your number one fan doesn't mean you are confident or cocky. It means you invest in yourself and set standards and goals above what anyone else would set for you. It means being able to walk in a room and tell people exactly what you can offer and why you are the best person for any position. You have to be able to articulate your experience, knowledge, skills, and worth in a way that will separate you from the rest. That is the X-Factor. In college is the best time to start creating your personal brand. You are in a place where you are already meeting thousands of new people for the first time, every year its new incoming freshmen that you can work and increase your brand and with the power of social media you have the time daily to build globally. If you want to be successful not only in college but in life, creating a personal brand isn't just an option, it's a necessity. Whether you aspire to get a promotion or

THIS IS WHY

land your dream job, creating a compelling and consistent brand will help you meet your goals.

In order to invest in yourself you have to be prepared for everything. Creating your brand isn't as hard as you may think. It just takes applying everything in my methods thus far. Here are eight specific steps to creating a personal brand based off applying my *New Face Method for Success.*

Step 1. (KEY# 2) The Intangibles. Do all the things that require zero talent great. Be likable and get your name out there by joining organizations working with people and becoming a leader. Paying attention to details, body language, how you look, and positive energy is important while creating your personal brand

Step 2. Know yourself set goals and plans specific to branding yourself. Think about what separates you from your peers. Know your strengths and weaknesses. Know what others think about you and why you are different.

Step 3. (Key #1) Those S. M. A. R. T. Goals and 1/5/10 year plans are important for what your brand will be and what message you want to give.

Step 4. Identify your target Audience: Whom do you want to appeal to and what are your priorities? Remember it's nothing wrong with multi-tasking but you must prioritize and have a plan as to what's most important and who are your target markets.

Step 5. Have your paperwork on point. That includes having a business card, up to date resume and activities resume. You never know whom you will meet at any moment. (More details in the next section in this chapter)

Step 6. The internet and social media is your best friend. Be on point with social media and have a website. Create a consistent website about you and your brand. Make sure it is primarily about you and not other people or organizations. Same with all social media outlets, Facebook, Instagram, twitter, etc., update daily and about your brand message. As I said earlier, in college you have the time to do these things. Take advantage. Blogging and podcasts are very popular now; think about what you can post weekly on blogs and podcasts while focusing on your skill set and experience. Create! Create! Create! If you really have time think about publishing a book.

THIS IS

Step 7. (key#6) Network Marketing. I will talk about this more later but when it comes to branding everyone you are associated with should know what you bring to the table. Always promote yourself. There is power in a network and communicating. Physically go out to meet people and socialize. Being a familiar face and being seen in person is just as important as social media. Social media is to expand your reach to people you hardly see if ever but never forget about the thousands of people you have right in front of you in college.

Step 8. Always follow up and do your research. There is nothing wrong with making adjustments and trying different approach if they way you brand yourself isn't working the way you expected.

For more information on the steps to personal branding be sure to contact me at yancy@newfacemanagement.org

THIS IS WHY

Business Cards

A business card even with social media and the way people have phones on their hip is STILL something that everyone looks for in the professional world. When I was in college, I had business cards at eighteen-years-old, my freshman year, and every year after. I go to speaking events now and people still ask for my business card. I remember recently, a panelist looking at me with a face of disappointment because I didn't have one on me at the time. Your business card shows people that you are a professional at what it is you do, even if it's just being a college student. Having a business card with your name, phone number and professional email address is all you need. Your professional email should be your name or your business name nothing cute and fancy UNLESS your business name calls for it. If you provide a service, have a website and a professional social media account.

Your social media professional account should include your name or business name. It's ok if you social media account isn't professional as a college student. Just don't put it on your business card. Be cautious about what you post. This is very important. Professional athletes, cops, political leaders and business owners have lost hundreds of thousands of dollars, friends and family due to social media posts, old and new. Once you post something even if you delete it, the post can be found. It's very important to learn this now and apply it moving forward. As a college student you can ruin potential opportunities by making irresponsible posts and photos. When it comes to your physical business card be mindful that people look at your social media as well.

www.Vistaprint.com is a great option to use to get bulk business cards for an inexpensive price.

Resume

One of the first things I ask my college interns is to send their resume along with a cover letter. A resume is a formal way of presenting yourself. You will see an example resume and cover letters at the end of this section submitted by a couple of my interns. A resume is a snapshot of what you have done up to that point in your life. A resume should relate to the field you are interested in pursuing and/or the job you are applying for at the time. Even if you are looking to be an entrepreneur where you don't work for anyone, there will be a time where some may ask for your resume so that they can have a "snapshot" of

THIS IS

what you have done up to this point. A resume shows your qualifications along with your educational background. You should always have a physical copy and a saved copy available that you can email upon request. Trust me, YOU NEVER KNOW. I've had situations where I was talking to someone about my goals and they asked for a copy of my resume for themselves or to pass along to someone else. It may not even be for a job, but it's a great tool to be able to show off your talent without having to speak.

Linkedin is another key to success in todays world. Linkedin is the professional facebook. It is your resume on line. Be sure to set up your linkedin account and keep it very professional. You will be able to connect with people and Business professionals will be able to reach out to you. Your linkedin account should reflect your resume and you on the most professional way possible weather you are starting your business, looking for an internship or searching for employment. All of my interns needed to have this as well.
www.linkedin.com

THIS IS WHY

Example Resumes
Imani J. Dunn

LinkedIn Profile: https://www.linkedin.com/in/imani-dunn-3bbb55b1/

Education

AUGUST 2014 – MAY 2019

B.A. in Communications / *Old Dominion University, Norfolk, VA (GPA: 3.2)*
Graduate: May 2019

Skills

- Interpersonal Communication Skills
- Superior Customer Service
- Leadership and Organizational Skills
- MICROS register proficiency
- Flexibility and Adaptability
- Strong Analytical Skills
- Decision Making Skills
- Microsoft Office Proficiency

Experience

SEPTEMBER 2018 – NOVEMBER 2018

Overnight Merchandising Supervisor / *American Eagle Outfitters, Norfolk, VA*

- Provide logistical expertise export shipments
- Assist store managers in the training and education of new hires
- Monitor workflow and inventory storage
- Expedite daily shipping work orders
- Serve as the sole support staff for all managers, directors, assistant directors, and assistants

THIS IS

FEBRUARY 2016 – PRESENT

Retail and Extra Charge Supervisor / *Cedar Fair Kings Dominion, Doswell,*
VA

- Led Customer service team and Information Center
- Manage up to 10-person team on variety of sales/retail initiatives
- Upsell merchandise and promotional items for events
- Use the G.A.M.E.R. Initiative and Operation Captivate to provide guests with the best experience possible
- Worked public relations

Leadership and Involvement

President – Caribbean Student Association (2016-2017); Chapter President – The Omega Chapter of Sigma Lambda Upsilon/Señoritas Latinas Unidas Sorority, Inc. (May 2017 – Present); Secretary – The Multicultural Greek Council (Spring 2018 – Present); Mentor – Life Enrichment Center (October 2017 – March 2018); Secretary and Treasurer – Success Without Limitations (February 2018 – Present); Order of Omega (December 2018)

THIS IS WHY

Nailah Sutherlin
Intern

Email- (insert) phone-(insert)

Professional Summary
I am a third-year Strategic Communication major with a strong interest in the
position of creative development and advertising for the entertainment industry. I possess eminent leadership skills, brand marketing strategies, the ability
to speak publicly and maintain control and influence over large crowds. I am
able to bring further insight from web design, critical and analytical thinking as
well as the skill of organization and artistic creativity.

Objective:
My goal with your company is to develop and enhance my current skills while
reciprocating that experience through my work.
I will be a dedicated leader exemplifying an efficient work ethic as I contribute
to the company through my creativity and
ideas.

Education
Hampton University | BA in Strategic Communications
July 2016 - May 2020

Experience

College Hive | Marketing Intern
Oct. 2016 - Nov. 2016

- Developed and improved the content strategies for the newly devel-
  oped application
- Conducted weekly seminars to discuss the progression
- Networked with the student body to expand our audience

Brand 757 | Creative Developer
Sep. 2017-Present

THIS IS

- Re-developed the new brand and content strategy for the relaunch of the company.
- Created several different proposals for our E-Board.
- Organized and lead weekly meetings with and for the company's members.

Student Leadership Program | Member
July 2017-Present

- Planned and oversaw on-campus events.
- Participated in community service events within the Hampton Roads community
- Created event proposals for our week of Springfest .

PRSSA | E-Board Member December
Dec. 2018 - Present

- Introduced and created our first event for the semester to bring in new members to the organization
- Lead an E-Board meeting for current and new members
- Organized sub-committee groups to help structure the execution of our event(s)

Skills

Media relations, Media management, MS Office, MS Word, MS Excel, Photoshop, InDesign, Reliability, Organizational Skills, Extrovert, Positive, Open-Minded, Persuasive, Innovator, Ambitious.

THIS IS WHY

Cover letter

A cover letter is very simple. It's just a letter introducing yourself and the information you sending a long with it. Now I always make my cover letters unique to the person or organization to whom I am sending it. The introduction will typically be the same: one to two sentences introducing yourself and explaining why you are sending the resume or other information.

"Good afternoon Mrs. Smith. This is Yancy Merchant. We spoke briefly the other day about my company, New Face Management, llc. I wanted to thank you for taking the time out after the panel to discuss some future ideas."

Three sentences provide a quick introduction and a refresher of who you are and what the cover letter is about. The body will give information about what you are sending. I like to give a little information about myself in relation to what they may do. This shows that you look a little time to find out about the person or business; and now you made it more personal.

"I attached my resume for you to review. I also took a look at your website and noticed you mentor teenagers. That is something I have a passion for as well. I really feel that teenagers need as many positive role models as possible in order to succeed. If you are available this week, I would like to set a time where we can discuss some opportunities where I can learn from you."

Very simple, but it gives the person an overview of your request and an opportunity for your personality to show.   The conclusion is comprised of one or two simple sentences:

Once again, thank you for your time. I hope to hear from you soon.

That is basically all you need for a cover letter. As you get more experience and when the situations present themselves, you will have to add more information.

Internships

An internship is a position a student or trainee takes with an organization, business, or company with or without pay to gain knowledge in a particular field and, in some circumstances, earn credit for graduation and/or qualifications for another position.

I am a father. I have been a high school teacher. I have been a youth football coach; I am a basketball coach now. I am a mentor and, soon, I will be starting college tours with my network. These are all things I can do to make a change in the world and inspire our youth to do better in their lives. There is no monetary value on that type of change. As a college student and a leader amongst my peers, I was a mentor to as many people as I could handle. I had over 100 interns. Some were able to graduate because of their work with me. Back then, I was just happy to help and grateful for all of them. Now, not only am I grateful and happy, I am proud to have been able to offer that service to college students who are trying to graduate just like I was.

Never underestimate the value of internships during undergrad and graduate studies in building your skills and professional network. Yes, most of them don't pay, but the skills you gain from getting hands-on experience in your field of study is invaluable and will pay dividends when you get into the workforce. Also, remember to nurture those relationships built during an internship. One of those people may become your mentors. Some may be able to provide recommendations when you are applying for jobs.

If you make a decision to own your own business consider providing internships or employing others. Giving internships and paid jobs to your peers is a big responsibility. You have to be able to balance friendship and your expectations so that they respect your authority as their boss. Make sure that you only hire and sponsor people who can handle the responsibilities and meet the requirements.

.

THIS IS WHY

Ashley Montgomery 2010 Graduate, New Face Scholarship recipient and current MBA Candidate at the University of Illinois at Chicago wanted to give her advice her advice on Internships:

"Start early! Many people will say that college students "don't intern until their Junior year."
Don't approach your life like that. Everything is about relationships and rapport. You should
start joining organization, networking, and applying for internships your freshman year (yes
applying). It may or may not lead to internship right away—maybe it will lead to a summer
program instead or just give you experience in interviewing to better seal the deal for next
summer. Either way—the grind is worth it. Internships lead to jobs. Start early and don't take
seeking an internship lightly."

Here are a few of my past interns:

Shante' Steward experienced firsthand what it is like to be friends with someone who runs the business where you work. She graduated in 2009 because of her internship with New Face:

"I want to start off by saying that New Face Entertainment literally changed my life. The organization changed my way of thinking and how I maneuvered throughout my duration in college as well as how I currently function and interact with people. The greatest thing that I learned from New Face was the word loyalty. People think they are loyal and they usually are to, maybe, their close friends and family. However, in the business world, there is a level of respect and loyalty that involves a balance of learning and mature obedience.

Yancy may have a different memory of this particular story, but this is how I remember it in short. After I worked as a Street Team member and a Co-Director, I became his paid Personal Assistant. There were about, maybe, three paid individuals on his team and I was one of them, which brings an even greater level of responsibility and loyalty. It was not just fun and games and being a party promoter at this point. I was called to step up and I was honored.

THIS IS

So, New Face had an event and I could not attend because I had a lot of work and studying to do. A lot of my friends, some who were on the New Face Street Team, decided not to go to the New Face party as well for various reasons. At some point, during the night, I got my homework and studying done and everybody decided to go to an Omega Psi Phi party. We got to the party late and didn't stay long, but a lot of people were at this particular party that should have been at the New Face party, not just because we ran the parties in the area and had great turnouts, but because we worked for New Face.

I remember there either being a meeting called or our regular weekly meeting in an auditorium style classroom on the grounds of Hampton University. Everyone took their seats and Yancy made a speech about how he saw us there and that we were wrong. I will leave it at that. However, then he begins to call out our names one-by-one and let us know that we were at that time, fired and released from the company. There were so many of us and I was in shock, but I know he was disappointed in us as well. That may not have hit home for some people, but it hit home for me and I took it personally. I did not think that going to another party, at the time, was wrong, but it absolutely was. Not only was I getting paid, but this was my friend, my boss and a company that I respected and was honored to be in. When my work was complete, I should've been at our party and not a Greek party.

From then on, I thought about the word loyalty. Even though it was not my intent to hurt anybody or seem as though I was not loyal to the brand and the organization, that is what it was. If I wanted to go to a Greek party on the same night that I was supposed to be working, then I should've been there or said something. The thought never entered my mind.

The way I functioned in college and thereafter stemmed from that one particular incident. I know what it is to be loyal to an organization. It is everything regardless of what people may think of how Yancy handled the situation, it has taught me so many lessons in life.

Working in New Face also started my love for marketing and promotions. I worked in radio for four years while attending Hampton and I was also the Promotions and Urban Promotions Director at the station, WHOV 88.1 FM. I knew that after college, communications, events and marketing is exactly where I wanted to be. I did have a short stint in trying to pursue my acting and singing career, but I don't believe that is where God wanted me to be. He wants

THIS IS WHY

me to be working in environments where I can uplift and help people. I believe I did that with New Face and I am doing that now."

"In order to graduate from HU, an internship in the music industry was required, and I was fortunate enough to have a Hampton Big Brother who owned a thriving entertainment company called New Face. During this semester long internship, I learned the Ins and outs of live Deejaying, enhanced my production skills, assisted in recording multiple mixtapes, and helped promote events, all while building lasting relationships."-Dominique Wilkins 2007 college graduate

THIS IS

Internship Letter of appreciation
Mr. Yancy Merchant
CEO of New Face Entertainment

Dear Mr. Yancy Merchant,

I am writing this letter to simply say thank you for all that you and New Face Entertainment has done for me. It is difficult to express how much I appreciate and truly value the experience that I have learned within the three years that I was with the company.

As you know I started off as an intern distributing promotional material to various campuses. Later gaining your trust to handle many of the financial transactions for special events and became secretary in my second year. Though it was not until my third year with the company when you promoted me to a director that I felt my hard work and dedication paid off. With the responsibilities of managing a street team of 10-15 people, writing press releases, media alerts, supervising photography shoots and developing marketing strategies I felt prepared for a field in management. Due to the opportunity that you provided I was able to use my last year with the company as a credited internship course at Hampton University. This was a class that was required in able to graduate from the School of Journalism and Communications.

Once again thank you for making my college experience meaningful along with making the workplace both fun and professional. It was a pleasure working with you and I wish nothing but success with your future endeavors.

Thanks Again,
Crystal S. Neal

THIS IS WHY

Scholarships/sponsorships

When I was an undergrad and graduate student, I had the honor of being able to offer scholarships to my interns called the *New Face Scholarship*. Every semester, we chose at least two students to receive money for school. Some scholarships were done through an application process; others were done through the internship. There were different criteria. Some funds were to be used for books, some were used to pay for tuition, and some were used to sponsor participation in campus life activities such as Greek organizations. At the end of this section are a couple of recipient testimonials.

I take pride in being able to give out scholarships, but I was also able to develop an internship program. It was an intense program built to provide mentorship to college students and teach them how to be successful in not only in their chosen fields but in life. Many of my interns needed this internship to graduate from various colleges along the East Coast. We gave out over $10,000 in scholarship money as a company to high school and college students. If you are in a position to give back, it is incumbent upon you to do so.

One of the first recipients of *New Face Scholarship* was Carl Gray, III a 2005 graduate political science major from Largo, MD. Carl Grey received a $1,000 sponsorship on behalf of my company to complete is last year and graduate. Without that he would not have received his degree. He received his scholarship because of his active roll with the company and passion he had to help the business become successful.

"I remember it was my last year at Hampton. I needed to make the requisite deposit to pay for school. I knew my parents were tapped out and I was completely "loaned" out. I didn't even want to ask for help. I was going to figure it out somehow...I have that "hustler's" mentality. If I remember correctly, I just happened to mention it to Yancy; not asking, or even expecting any assistance. He immediately said, "We got you, big bro." And within a matter of hours, I had the funds needed. It was about $1,000, and I was assuming it was a loan. However, my lil bro – yes <u>little</u> brother informed me to just consider it a scholarship. Honestly, I think I was the first recipient of a "New Face Scholarship" It was key to me finishing that semester."

Jessica McKenzie was a recipient from White Plains, NY and is a 2007
graduate political science major Spanish minor.

*"The New Face Scholarship provided financial assistance ($500) to stu-
dents who have exhibited academic excellence, exemplary leadership
and passion that blazed a trail for others to follow to positively impact
their local community. The New Face Scholarship was a full circle moment for me because here we were as students a part of the New Face
family hosting events that brought everyone together — every race,
creed, cultural background — and brought unending joy to our college
community; and then a portion of earnings was reverted into a*

scholarship to help us as students. This gesture resonated with me

*because it created this virtuous circle of an organization valuing their
members and contributing to them excelling academically. I believe New
Face lasted well beyond when I graduated because at its core it was
more than just hosting unforgettable events, it was about developing the
next generation of well-rounded leaders."*

Ashley Montgomery 2008 recipient on winning the New Face Scholarship:

*"I was a recipient of the New Face Scholarship in 2008 or 2009. What drew
me to apply was the fact that the requirements were so out of the box. I had to
write a brief statement, but the main component was to provide referrals. I had
not participated in other scholarships because of the daunting monotony of
writing yet another paper while in school (don't be like me—get all the money
you can, so that you can have financial freedom post-graduation), but the New
face scholarship was out of the box and kind of fun! I can picture myself now--
in the library cranking out those referrals and thinking "I hope I win AND this
better be legit!" Needless to say, I won, and it was legit. I remember the quick
follow up from the owner, Yancy, to release the money. I was impressed by the
turnaround time, professionalism, and genuine excitement of me winning. The
scholarship was truly right on time and I am still grateful to this day."*

THIS IS WHY

Create Something

What is most important to me is to change the world. I want to leave as many imprints as possible. The whole world doesn't have to know you changed the world, either. One of my close friends, artist and activist Karega Bailey, once told me that I have residual impact. He felt I have a tendency to create things that have a lasting effect long past the time they were implemented.

He told me what it meant to him that I can create ideas and leave a foundation for others to continue and build on leaving an impact for years and decades to come.

One example of residual impact from college is something we call the "12-2". The "12-2" is an event that takes place in the student center at Hampton University. A DJ comes in during the hours of 12-2 and plays music while different organizations host events. If you talk to students now, it's still one of the biggest events that takes place on campus. Students plan their class schedules around the 12-2 to make sure they don't miss anything. Everyone from current students to alumni and people visiting from other colleges knows to come to the student center during that time to socialize and find out about upcoming events. The 12-2 has been going on since 2003 before having Day Parties was even a "thing".

The 12-2 is an event that now has a lasting effect and has permanent residency at Hampton University. The history of how and why the 12-2 was created is an interesting one. My freshman year was 2001-2002, the same year the student center was built.

When we had DJs come on campus, they played outside near the cafeteria, dorms, and the president's house. Sean, Howard, and I didn't have our own sound and DJ equipment, yet. We were using car sub speakers and house speakers for parties; we rented equipment for our "big" events from companies like All City Entertainment. All City is run by DJ VINCE, another great man and business owner, by the way.

In the summer of 2003, Monet Clements was President of the student union board and we received our first major on-campus contract to provide DJ services on for every event SUB hosted. We were juniors in college now given the task to provide services for over 30 events for the year, but there were no events during the hours of 12-2pm. That came about because of the "storm" part of this perfect storm. Hurricane Isabel hit the Hampton Roads area in September of 2003 only a couple weeks after the semester began. It was one of the worst hurricanes in history. Some students were able to get home, and some weren't. The students that were unable to leave the area had to seek refuge either off campus or on campus in the University gym. Sean, Howard and I lived off campus and had over 15 people staying with us without any power. All we had was each other, a grill to cook, and fun. We made it work. We would go to campus to see how everyone was doing and try to come up with creative ways to boost morale. You can only imagine how people felt at the time without power. We had minimal areas to shower and a lack of personal space. Half of the student center had power. So, we brought in outside equipment during the day because at night there was a city wide curfew due to the power outage for over a week and a half. During the day, my company would come on campus and play music in the student center. Every day would turn into a day party. There was nothing else to do at the time but enjoy the moment and have fun.

Finally, power was restored on campus. We thought we should keep the momentum going. Since we already had a contract with the student union board, our own equipment, and consistent events off campus, it only made sense to try playing music during the day while classes were back in session. We started on Wednesdays and Fridays between 12-2pm…Then my fraternity brothers got on board throwing "Alpha Fridays" the first Friday of every month. Then 12-2 just took off from there. Omega Psi Phi and other fraternities and sororities reached out for our services as did other college organizations…Presently, 12-2 is one of the most popular events on campus.

(for personal stories on what the 12-2 meant to students and hurricane Isabel go to my website www.thisiswhydoc.com to view interviews for free)

Ryan "Boogie" Marsh played a big part in the growth of "12-2" as he was one of the biggest DJs on campus and he mentored newer DJs coming up after him leaving a major legacy without even knowing it. When we were roommates while I was in graduate school, I watched his talent in action. He taught DJs such as Megan Ryte who is currently on NYs Hot 97 as well as a list of other DJs in their beginning stages. He also had talents at that time that have matured

THIS IS WHY

into his current business. He used to have new, innovative ideas when he created designs for our events, just like he does now with his films and app development.

As college students, you have the world at your disposal. This is the time to come up with and create things that don't exist. Find those needs and fulfill them. No idea is a dumb idea. Take advantage of every situation and turn a negative into a positive. We could have just stayed in during hurricane Isabel. No one told us to come and play music, but look what it turned into. The campus would be totally different now over 15 years later had we not seized the opportunity the crisis presented.

In "The Secret," one of the topics is the "Law of Attraction." I truly believe in energy and attracting like minds and people. We all feed off each other and can bring out gifts that we see in others. I am not the only person in my network that created things in college and either made money or built it into something successful after graduation. Innovators are the inventors and re-inventors of the world. I want you to think like and become innovators. I want you to think about ways to improve ideas and create some of your own. If you are constantly creating new ideas, over time a few will catch on. That is how you begin to build and create long-term wealth.

Here are others who were able to capitalize on ideas they had in college or even as early as high school.

Justin Sharpe (@justcobar) is currently a Business Management Major at Hampton University from Baltimore, MD. Justin has been a professional photographer and videographer since the age of 16. He first began learning his craft in high school by way of a digital photography course. As the course went on, his teacher expressed that he saw "raw talent" in Justin, and that if he let him teach him, he could be something special and make some money. Justin first started shooting his high school's basketball games, then candid photos around school. Soon thereafter, prom send offs, senior portraits, and graduation parties became regular gigs. As more exposure came and he began to perfect his craft, he took over his high school's yearbook and made major changes. Also, he became head of his school's twitter account because of his knowledge of social media marketing and branding. Now at 20 years old, Justin is very experienced in his craft. Some of his best work is his studio fashion photography work. He also was the main photographer for the annual "in-the- industry" panel I hosted on campus. Events are one of his favorite subjects to shoot because of his ease of interaction with people. Justin also has a passion for fashion consulting and is looking to pursue personal shopping as a new venture.

Chris Queen is currently my website developer. In college, he was a computer science major and he and his friends created The Paparazzis. They saw a need to document events, including mine, on campus. They filled a need, and to this day I am grateful. He has documentation of the majority of my events from that time period. This was a time before social media. He made it easy to preserve the pictures that chronicled our journey. Now, Chris owns his own software development company and built my current website

www.newfacemanagement.org

Conrad Llewellyn was in college when he started working in a car shop and ended up owning his own. He worked on all my cars and company vans while I was in college.

THIS IS WHY

Norshon Sheridan is a promoter and business partner of mine. He started doing events in college and has expanded his business up the East Coast doing Spring Break, Homecoming, and Labor Day events. He has planned events in places like Miami, North Carolina, New York, and Cancun.

James "Cali" Callahan, Norfolk State alumni, promoter, and business partner created the So Phocused brand and expanded it into a new company called El Capitan. He manages artists, has a clothing line, and inspires youth by mentoring and doing public speaking engagements in schools and after-school programs in California.

Chris Roy was a part of my company for a while then went on to own his own event planning company while in college. He then expanded to Miami and is now in California. He's one of the biggest promoters in Southern California as the owner and CEO of The Lifestyle Agency.

Crystal Neal was a member of New Face and used the company to create ideas she had and wanted to work on such as the New Face beauties. I always wanted people to take an interest in the company and come up with ideas to create their own. Crystal did that on a number of occasions. New Face Beauties was a Calendar book she created. Jack Manning who is currently a photographer and director assisted in the production and photo shoot. Crystal used her networks to do choreography with various organizations and helped put together events for me such as YOU got served, a dance competition where different dance crews along the East coast were able to compete and perform in front of over 1,000 people.

Broadway Chapman and Clay west changed beauty pageants and fashion shows on campus along with their vision of what they wanted pageants and Fashion shows to look like. As college students, they were given the task to complete fashion shows and pageants. They added modern day walks down the runway, music, and new choreography, which paved the way for future shows and pageants for the years to come on their campus.

Nick Mitchell from NY, NY, a graduate of Hampton University and a brother of Beta Gamma Chapter of Phi Beta Sigma Fraternity Inc., saw the need for a pep team at Hampton. As a student body, before Nick and his friends, we didn't have the usual team spirit you would see on a college campus. We didn't have the students wear body paint running up and down the stands during games to get the school excited for games. Nick was one of those people that saw the need and filled it. Prior to Nick and his friends, there was a very small team spirit.

"We helped give it importance and a strong backing. Without me, Josh Crenshaw (brother of the Gamma Iota chapter of Alpha Phi Alpha Fraternity, Inc.), AJ Council (brother of the Beta Chi chapter of Kappa Alpha Psi, Fraternity Inc.,) pushing boundaries, it would have been small lackluster group of students. It was our 3 to paint our bodies and get administrator to pay for it."
-Nick Mitchell

Marvin Ganthier, a freshman in 2005 at Hampton University, was one of my DJs and did a great job at his craft. But I saw more in Marvin and, unlike Tay, he needed more of a push in the business. I wanted to show him that he was more than just a DJ. I saw he had potential to be a business owner and had a following of his own with a team that supported him no matter what. I decided to put him in a leadership position in the company where he was able to manage his own interns. That taught him responsibility and leadership while still working on his craft. It gave him the opportunity to learn how to run a business and make tough decisions. He was able to take that experience and knowledge to build his own brand. Now, he's one of the most well known DJs in the DC area. He has an annual summer event with those same friends from college known as the BAFC (Big Ass F*uckin Cookout). This event is one of the most anticipated events every summer. People travel to Maryland every year to go to an undisclosed location, partying with friends, eat great food all day, and have a blast.

These are all examples I wanted to give you so that you can see that this isn't just unique to me. This is not something that just happens during a certain period or at one or two universities. You can do similar things anywhere. You just have to be motivated and don't just talk about ideas but do them.

THIS IS WHY

I am not here to tell you to dropout of school to start a business. I am here to tell you, you can create anything you want while still in school learning the tools in the classroom and applying them outside the classroom. You have an idea? You have a vision? Don't wait until you graduate to get it going. Start it now. Talk to your peers. Research what other people have done that may be similar to your ideas. See how you can do it differently. Develop a plan and get it going. Sit back and take the time to decide what you want to do and how to do it.

THIS IS

You can develop something and begin to change the world. It's a fact that entrepreneurship and investing in real estate can be key components to a plan for building wealth. Start owning a business at an early age. You will have better control of your financial future. In order to do that, you have to create a clear idea of what your business is and what direction you're going. One of the themes of this book is finding what you're passionate about and following your dreams, ideas and goals. But another theme is to have a plan. That is one of my mottos. Develop a business plan so you can easily present it to potential investors and people who want to know more about your business. Here is a basic outline from money crashers that can help you get started.

Mission Statement: "A mission statement communicates the ultimate purpose of your business idea and details how you intend to operate and grow.

Development of Resources: What resources do you currently have at your disposal (skill set, home office, marketing channels) and what resources do you have to acquire and further develop. What do you expect the cost in time and money to be?

Profit and Loss Forecast: Create a monthly picture of your expected income and expenses over the first 12 to 24 months of your venture. The sooner you feel you can reach profitability, the better. But don't sugarcoat your projections at all; An honest assessment is critical at this stage.

Proposed Product/Service Development: How do you intend to go from the idea phase to a finished product or service? You need a concrete plan for how you're going to develop your product or service, how much it will take to get there, and who will aid in the effort.

Marketing Strategy: How do you intend to reach customers? Thanks to the Internet, social media marketing is an excellent tool. Create pages on Facebook, Twitter, Instagram, and additional platforms. Reach customers by engaging them on your competitors' pages. Start a blog and optimize your use of keywords to draw attention to your business. You have to be relentless in your efforts to create a client base.

THIS IS WHY

Financial Literacy and Money Management

When you start thinking about building a business, financial literacy and knowing how to manage your money is very important. Financial literacy is knowing how money is made, spent and saved. It's also the ability to use the money you have to make good financial decisions such as spending, saving, and investing.

I wasn't educated in financial literacy the way I should have been at 18 years old. That is why I am informing all of you now so that you will be aware and make better decisions than I did. I had between $50,000 and $100,000 dollars a year from 18-25. If I had improved my financial literacy back then, I would be in a much better financial situation now. I want you to be able to set yourself up to be financially secure at an early age. It can happen before you know it!

I knew nothing about a credit report and its effect on my adult life. If you do get a credit card, make sure you use it but pay it off every month. Make sure that the credit card is 5-10% used every month. For example, if you have a $500 credit card limit, every month to make sure the balance is below $50.

One of the things I didn't have in college was a credit card. You may hear different advice, but I suggest you actually get a credit card or two with low credit limits. That means that each card should not allow you to spend more than 500 to 1000 dollars. Paying on an active credit card allows you to establish a successful credit history, which will be important when you are ready to move on to other stages in your life. Use your credit card to pay for regular but smaller expenses like your phone bill or gas for the car that you can pay off right away.
Some parents and students prefer to have a debit card or cash card, instead. This is certainly an option that makes sense for people who are having trouble setting limits on themselves. But consider phasing this out and using a credit card as you learn to balance your money so that you can graduate with established credit.

I am a life coach and planner. I review budgeting with people. Learning to pay bills on time will save you from having a horrible credit score or living above your means. Use credit cards to establish credit; do not use credit cards to buy things you can't afford.

THIS IS

Be mindful of what we call predatory lenders who prey on college students by encouraging them to enroll in credit cards they can't afford. Also, avoid taking out more on your student loans than you need. Companies offer loans because they know you need the money. But, what sometimes happens is that students get deeply in debt. When you can't pay it back, your credit is destroyed. Trust me, I know. It takes years to get it back to a point where you are comfortable.

Start relying less on your parents for money, and learn to be self-sufficient. This is the time you learn how to stretch $20 over a week. Become resourceful. Establish credit at an early age. Parents, if you want to help your children, allow them to learn the value of their money by not rushing to bail them out of financial missteps that aren't an emergency. If they chose to buy new shoes instead of groceries, allow them to live with the consequences of that choice until their next payday. Help them by setting up a credit card, and teach them stay on track with paying it off on time and making monthly payments. I would definitely suggest looking into a financial literacy class in college and joining an organization related to finances, money management, and minimizing debt. There are some high schools pushing to make financial literacy and planning a required course as economics credit. If you've had one of these, you are ahead of the curve. Students need the critical, basic life skills to manage their money and plan for financial freedom.

There are various tutorials about financial literacy online. You can reach me via my website directly for basic information on money management and credit card responsibility. I also do budget consulting. Carrington Carter is a wealth strategist and is an excellent resource for more complex information. Carrington Carter helps people build wealth. For example, he gives advice about how to invest early over a long period of time in a high interest savings account and a low cost index fund. He does a great job of putting together different accounts that will maximize your dollars over different time frames (e.g., five years, 20 years).

THIS IS WHY

Carrington Carter, wealth strategist and entrepreneur, said this:

"We didn't talk about credit much in my household. I've always been a pretty responsible person. With the guidance of my parents, the first credit card I had was USAA credit card with a spending limit of $600. I was told to use it in case of emergency, don't spend out of control, and pay all your bills on time (credit card, cable, rent, cell phone, car payment, etc.) I was told that it's important to build credit and maintain good credit, but I taught myself how to leverage credit to build wealth. Credit education is significantly lacking in the African American community."

If you're interested in learning more about that, he can be reached at carrington.carter@gmail.com. Tell him I sent you.

If you start investing $100 a month in an index fund that has an average annual return of 7%, you can have approximately $18,000 by the time you are 30 years old starting at 18. Compounding interest allows that money to make even more money over time. You can go from tens of thousands of dollars to hundreds of thousands of dollars over a few decades of with minimal initial investing. Think about a long-term plan that includes building wealth by investing early and establishing credit.

Read the article found at https://www.cnbc.com/2019/03/01/nfls-brandon-copeland-is-teaching-life-101-a-money-class-at-Penn.html?__source=sharebar%7Cfacebook&par=sharebar

It features the financial class taught by NFL linebacker Brandon Copeland at Penn. The article speaks about the "50-30-20 rule" of personal finance, meaning 50 percent of income goes to necessities like rent and groceries, 30 percent towards discretionary spending and 20 percent towards saving. That's a great rule of thumb to go by while you are in college transferring from a teenager to an adult. Start thinking about ways to own your own company, properties and creating ideas that will build wealth for yourself. He, like myself, came up with the idea to teach because he wanted others to learn from the mistakes he made at an early age. I was making thousands of dollars every week in school. I did well, yes. But I could have done a much better job managing my money and planning ahead.

THIS IS

Tatiani Favors was one of my interns from Atlanta, Georgia that now owns her own company, Thrive Tax Systems, INC that teaches business, tax preparations, and accounting practices. She is able to give advice for college students looking to start their own businesses and change the world.

Financial responsibility while owning a business is critical! A goal of building my business was to get to a point where it was able to run itself. That requires appropriate funding. If you have made the decision to start a business, you will need start-up funds. There are multiple ways to obtain funds to start your company…let's explore some!

If you currently have a job, INVEST IN YOURSELF! Realize you are making the important decision of starting your own business. Every time you get paid, pay yourself. What does this mean? This means a portion of every check, a certain percentage or a flat amount, should be saved toward your goal.

RESEARCH! - If you know you would like to own your own company, do your due diligence and ensure you are aware of the necessary steps required to make your dream come to fruition.
- What are the steps?
- What do you need to keep the business going? (i.e. software, products, payroll, etc)
- How will you let everyone know that you are in business? (i.e. marketing)

How much does all that cost? Are there any FREE options that will suffice while in the building stage?

LOANS - Family members, Friends, Banks, Business Grants for start-ups… there are so many options to get money for a startup. All you have to do is look! If you are a minority, there are grants for you. A woman? There are grants for you. Also, look into government contracts in your state and see if your industry fits into one of the categories Apply. That is a significant way to jump-start your company.

MINDSET SHIFT! - Owning a company (and successfully expanding that company) requires a mindset shift in pretty much every aspect of your life (especially financial). In the words of Jim Rohn: "Income does not far exceed personal development. Sometimes income takes a lucky jump but unless you grow out where it is, it will usually come back where you are." This statement proves true if you look at individuals who have won the lottery and are dead broke a few years later, same for athletes

DON'T PLAY AROUND WITH COMPANY FUNDS! JUST SAY NO! JUST DON'T DO IT! - This is where self-discipline, a mindset shift, and personal development all come to work! Just because your company made $100, doesn't mean you have $100 to spend! Once your company begins to generate income, you must consider various expenses that are associated with the upkeep (and expansion) of your company. Do you have office space? Do you need wifi? Software? Payroll? Monthly/annual subscriptions? Do you utilize your vehicle and travel often? Do you require a certain look? Want to join any groups/trainings that will set you apart from your competition? These things cost money and are investments in your brand.

HAVE A COMPANY "POT"-Similar to the 'pay yourself first' model, you want to recycle funds back into your company. In the beginning, you may be paying for company expenses out of personal accounts. However, once you are established and earning income, ensure that you pay company expenses FIRST with that income. After a while, the company should be able to pay for its own expenses. If you spend the income first, you may not replace it in time to cover company expenses.

Invest in some type of accounting/bookkeeping system or hire a professional. As a business owner, your expertise is running your business. Many business owners do not specialize in bookkeeping or accounting nor do they know the inner workings of accounting. Best practice is to get someone who can summarize your company's financial situation so at any given moment you know and understand where your company stands, financially. This is done by producing and utilizing what is referred to as Financial Statements. There are many kinds of financial statements. The most popular kind and the one I recommend for new businesses is a Profit & Loss Statement. It's also known as an Income Statement. This statement lists all your company's income and expenses for a given time period (typically monthly & annually). Profit & Loss statements can answer questions such as: Did you make a profit? Are there expenses to consider cutting; what's your biggest income source. You never want to be unaware of your company's financial reality.

THIS IS

Merchant's New Face Method for Success
Take Home Notes:

- Follow my eight steps
- Look for internships that align with your brand and goals
- Have a resume business cards and cover letter template ready
- Create something
- Change the world don't just live in it
- If you want to start a business, create a business plan and go for it
- Be smart with your money
- Be financially responsible

THIS IS WHY

Merchant's New Face Method for Success
9 keys to be an Effective College Student outside the classroom

1 - IT'S TIME TO SET YOUR SCHEDULE (DAILY ROUTINE)
2 - PERFECT THINGS THAT REQUIRE ZERO TALENT IT'S TIME TO
SET YOUR SCHEDULE
3 - JOIN ORGANIZATIONS
4 - BE THE X FACTOR
5 - BRAND AND INVEST IN YOURSELF
6 - CREATE YOUR N.E.T.W.O.R.K.
7 - DEVELOP YOUR NEW FACE
8 - BE A SERVANT TO THE COMMUNITY
9 - ALWAYS REMEMBER "WE PROMOTE IT"

THIS IS

KEY #6 - CREATE YOUR N.E.T.W.O.R.K.

Inspirational Person: Carl Gray III
P.L.A.N.
There is Power in a Network
N.E.T.W.O.R.K
"You're Only as strong as your weakest link"
Communicate
Networking quotes
Take Home Notes
References

THIS IS WHY

Inspirational Person
Carl Gray III

Born in Washington, DC and Raised in Prince George's County, MD to Carl, Jr. & Shirley Gray, he has always had a great support system. Carl has been a faithful member of Integrity Church International his entire life and attributes much of his success to the training and love provided by his Pastor, Dr. Emma Jean Thompson.

Carl, who is a member of the class that is the 5th incarnation of the "Purest Most Concentrated Essence under the sun," QT5, has managed to leverage his time as a Student Leader, and the skills he acquired negotiating the Maze that is Hampton University, into two very successful careers since his matriculation through Hampton University.

Prior to becoming a Student Leader, Carl co-founded, along with Deidre Couey, the "Black Heritage Extravaganza" now known as BHX in 2001. As Student Leader, Carl received the Mark Brown/Kim Coleman "Most Outstanding Student Leader" award and the Student Leader "Agape Award". He was also the Co-Facilitator for the Group of "perfect completion" GROUP 7!

During Carl's time in Hampton, he was voted Mr., MDDC Pre-Alumni, the First Mr. Chi Eta Phi, Mr. Pi Sigma Alpha Political Science Honors Society and performed in two homecoming concerts as a Drummer For Hampton's own "Waterfront Harmony." During his sophomore year, Carl began his career in politics, consulting on political campaigns, which was his passion. Upon leaving Hampton, Carl continued in politics and played a key role in getting a number of politicians elected.

Eventually, Carl lost his desire to "play the political game" and used his connections to enter the realm of IT Security Consulting. Working for what was then the largest minority CPA firm in the Nation, Carl broke the record for becoming Senior Auditor, and IT Audit Manager. Amidst some trying times with the firm, Carl decided to branch off and start his own Management Consulting practice, Prototype Consulting Group, in 2013, which he still runs to this day. He served many Federal Government Administrations, as well as state and local governments. He helps businesses, small and large, to protect their information and streamline processes for increased profit and efficiencies. Prototype Consulting Group also helps startup entrepreneurs grow their businesses quick-

THIS IS

ly and take advantage of the methodologies that the "Big Boys" use to organically grow beyond expectations.

Carl is also the founder of the "Learn From A Hacker" educational series that teaches individuals, companies, and organizations how to protect themselves from the peril of the internet.

Carl is also an internationally published photographer and owner of "Prototype Promotions" which focuses on capturing, through photography, the most important moments in the lives of people, individuals, and companies. Carl has served the likes of George Clinton, Mary J. Blige, DoTERRA International, Callaloo Kids, and the Syncopated Ladies, just to name a few. Prototype Promotions also does brand consulting for startup businesses.

www.PrototypePromotions.com

IG: @ProtoPromo @LearnFromAHacker

THIS IS WHY

P.L.A.N.

*You need **P**roper **L**eadership to **A**ccess and create a strong **N**etwork*

~J. Yancy Merchant

N.ew partnerships and friends
E.ffective and efficient
T.alk "closed mouths don't get fed"
W.illing to actively listen
O.pen to communicate
R.eal honesty
K.eep building

~J. Yancy Merchant

THIS IS

<u>There is Power in a Strong Network</u>

I knew at a young age I wanted to be successful–whatever it was. I had been working since I was in high school and played multiple sports. In college I hit the ground running joining multiple organizations, starting a business my freshman year and working part time by my sophomore year I rarely needed to be told to stay busy. I stayed engaged doing things I wanted to do with friends who had the same interests. My closest friends were exactly the same Your network is very important as to which direction you will go in life. Your network, believe it or not, starts with your friends and extended family. They are your influencers outside of your home. Although you always need to have independent thinking to be a leader in life, it is paramount to build a network and lifelong friendships that support your goals. It may be on you to help shape your own friends into being successful leaders. Build each other up. That comes with the territory of being a leader. Motivate your network to be the best people they can be, and you will benefit each other.

I created two acronyms to help you to prepare your network beyond your family and close friends.

First, you need to P. L. A. N. You need Proper Leadership to Access and create a strong Network. I know I was put on this Earth to create leaders. That's my purpose. To prepare your network you need to be a leader. A follower can't take full advantage of a network. That means you need to step up in a number of ways. That means being the strongest person in the room. That means taking advice and learning from those before you. That means being a positive influence on your peers and those coming after you.

I don't know everything, but I do know different people that are capable of getting things done. People contact me all the time about the most random issues: working out, schools, businesses, stocks. I am not an expert in any one field, but I do know someone in nearly any field that will know what you need. I've been able to help people with various issues from graduating from college, to getting community service hours, to buying a house, to investing. You name it, I've been able to help someone with it. I have been able to connect people in order for them to be successful in their endeavors. All because of the network I have built and the strong relationships I have kept with people.

THIS IS WHY

Calling someone just to see how they are doing or supporting their ideas and businesses can go a very long way. Having an open ear to listen or give advice means a lot to anyone. Just being a genuinely good person goes a very long way. Being helpful and being a reliable person and a person of your word goes even farther.

Learning the art of networking and being able to utilize that network is very important while in college because of the number of people you meet from various backgrounds that end up spreading all over the world.

My love for being a people person slowly turned into becoming a motivator. A motivator is defined as a person who promotes interest in or enthusiasm for something. I never realized how much of a motivator I was until people started to tell me over and over again how I'd convinced them that they could move mountains. I knew I had a talent for putting people in a position for success. But over time, I realized I also knew who to bring together to build perfect teams for community service projects, special events, and business plans. This book is a good example. My plan to change the world will be another. It all takes proper planning and motivation along with a number of other factors that involve a strong network.

Carl Grey is one of the best people I met when it comes to not only utilizing his network to his full potential but being a leader as well. As I said before they go hand and hand. He built on his network throughout college and then was able to make his own decisions to move around as he made career changes, then went into business for himself. He was able to use what he learned in the class-room, what he learned outside the classroom, and his strong network to be successful.

THIS IS

N.E.T.W.O.R.K.

I heard someone once say "If you want to go fast, do it alone. If you want to go far, do it together." Building a network is not something that happens overnight and it's not something that you can do alone. So exactly what does NETWORK mean? A Network, to me, is a group of people you can reach out to gather information, to build off of, to create success. Not everyone in the network has the same goals and every person's network is different from another because everyone is associated with different people on different levels. We may know the same people but my relationship with them may be totally different. I may know backgrounds and abilities of people that you may have no idea about. Below, I broke down the word NETWORK to give you better direction as to what you need to do to build your network.

New partnerships and friends

You can't have a network without people. Go out to events. Use social media. Look for people and partnerships that are mutually beneficial. While in college, you have thousands of people at your disposal that are the same age and similar goals. Use that to your advantage and get to know new people. You are always taking a risk putting yourself out there. But remember what I said about risk in X factor section four? It's needed! College is the time to take risks, meet new friends, and building new partnerships. When you join organizations, it is important to be social and increase your network of friends that will become potential business partners and a part of your new extended family.

Effective and Efficient

Don't just meet new people and let that be it. Don't just say, "Hey, nice to meet you," exchange information and walk away. Follow up. Spend time together. Brainstorm about everything, including non-business related topics. Have fun together. Get to know people on a personal level.

THIS IS WHY

T*alk. "Closed mouths don't get fed."*

Pick each other's brains. You never know what can happen from a conversation. Speak up. Talking can go a long way. Always stay in contact; do not lose people in your network .This is where I feel like practicing public speaking can be important, as well. Most universities offer classes on public speaking. Take advantage and use that class to become a better networker. Learn how to speak up and speak properly. Public speaking is one of the most common fears for people. Taking a class AND joining organizations where you have to speak in front of your peers and present ideas and plans is a great way to grow and learn.

W*illing to actively listen*

Being an active listener is very important when building a network. I discussed this earlier. It is very important to understand that people give out information about themselves and their goals and abilities all the time. If you don't actively listen, how will you be able to retain the information said? Being an active listener is an area where customer service people often excel. Someone has an issue or wants to discuss something with you. In order to properly understand what it is they are talking about, you have to listen and pay attention. It is very difficult to listen when you have a preset answer in your brain before you even hear the issue. Clear your head and listen to the people or person and respond based on the information you hear. This may require some critical thinking and conflict resolution in order for things to be resolved. That a good thing because those are the type of issues that require you to learn and get experience dealing with people within your network when things aren't on the of terms.

O.*pen to communicate*

I cannot begin to tell you how relationships can be lost because of not communicating. Everything won't be perfect at all. It's impossible for everything to go according to plan but always keep the lines of communication open. Be a person of your word. If you say you're going to do something, do it. If you feel like you can't do it in time or at the original time you said you were to get it done, keep the lines of communication open. No one is perfect, but simple things like this keep relationships strong. It took me a long time to learn humility. There are people right now who don't know it's easy to just make a phone call and talk to resolve a conflict.

THIS IS

R.*eal honesty*

Honesty is the best policy. You will have people in your network that you rely on and they will rely on you. Be honest with each other. Allow people to appreciate and internalize information to decide what part they can play in your network. Their roles may change as your network grows and expands over time but honesty should never change.

K*eep building*

Lastly, continue to grow and build your network. You can never have enough people in your network. Learning how to manage people is a goal. As your network grows, it will be second nature managing the people in your life. The more people you meet and get to know for business and personal purposes, the better. Maintain those relationships and treat people right. You never know. Later, I will talk more about being a mentor. But keep in mind that as you get older, there will be younger people that will look to you as a mentor. You will be an important part of their networks and it will be your turn to put them in the best position to be successful.

Continue to surround yourself with like-minded people, younger and older, who are inspired and motivated. The more open-minded you are, the more opportunities you will receive. I want you to be grateful for everything you receive from your new family and passionate about whatever it is you believe in and build off that energy.

THIS IS WHY

"You're only as strong as your weakest link."

Not everyone deserves to be in your network. The people you surround yourself with are a reflection of you. Sometimes, you have to push people within your network to be better than what they are because they may not realize their potential. You can't have people around you with opposite goals or those who aren't looking to move ahead in life. It's a tough pill to swallow, but sometimes your friends won't do the right thing no matter how much you try to motivate them and get some positivity out of them. You may have to consider minimizing your time with that person and directing your energy in another direction in order for you to grow more.

If your weakest link is working on their craft and doing their best to move in the right direction, it's up to the rest of the network to put that link in the best position possible to be successful. Not everyone can be the MVP but a team can't win without the role players. In many ways, the network you build in College will become your family. Some people, over time will become closer to you than your actual family. And there is absolutely nothing wrong with that as long as the intentions are pure and mutual. It's important to choose wisely, be aware of your intentions and the intentions of others. The people you go to college with will end up your lifelong friends. They will be the ones you go on trips with, invite to be in your wedding, confide in. They are also the ones you will fight with and make up with years later. Your college family will be the ones who will sculpt you into the person you are in your mid to late 20/30s without you even realizing it. I personally built my network like family because that's what I needed in college. I used to cook for my college family, business partners, line brothers, and roommates all the time. I wanted to have that kind of bond with people and for them to know our relationships weren't all about business all the time. I always want the closest people in my network to be people I can call for nearly anything at any time.

Just to give an example of the power of networking and the potential of how things happen within my network alone, I am producing my documentary and this book "in house" from beginning to end. I didn't have to outsource at all. All I had to do was reach out to my network because I had a vision and got the job done. Putting together an idea of this magnitude takes time and effort. I always say that anything can be done with proper planning no matter what it is and "If you want to do it fast do it alone if you want to do it long do it together." This is just a hint of what a network can do and what my network

THIS IS

has done for me. It just gives you a look ahead of what happens when you maintain relationships over the years. Everyone grows together. I plan to write a whole book on the power of networking as a part of a three part series that includes this book.

Sheronda Lawson, Esq is went to Hampton University and is the attorney for my company. I've known her since 2002 when she was a member of my original street team, making proposals for campus events Rachel Preston and Tamera Sease, two friends who majored in English always helped me with my business proposals by editing; which was never my strong point. They both have helped me over time with personal and business editing. Tamera is currently one of my book coaches and Rachel has given me advice…for this publication. Bill Mitaritonna is my High school basketball coach who has been helping me throughout this process. He even bought me the book published by Chandler Bolt that has helped get me through the writing process.

Karson Austin, the Vice President for New Face Entertainment, llc in college, was a finance major. He was a perfect fill-in when Sean and Howard moved on in their careers. I can rely on all three of them to do exactly what I need to be done when I'm not present. All three are Godfathers to my children, by the way. It's the same Karson that helped with the intangibles in Key #2. Dr. Howard Crumpton wrote a review for this book as psychologist along with Sean's wife Jessica, who is also a writer and motivator. Sean was also the best man in my wedding while Howard and Karson were groomsmen.

Chris Queen created the Paparazzi in college, a group that became responsible for the majority of the pictures and video for my events. He also played a major role as a computer science major to get Facebook open on Hampton University campus. He assisted with my website while we were in college. Presently, he owns his own company and built my current website along with my long time friend Ralph Oliver. Ralph Oliver has been my little brother since 2002. We have worked on various business throughout the years. He recently has helped with rebranding my company logo and help with the T-shirt design for Success without Limitations at ODU. Ralph through his businesses, has also helped me not only with my website but the branding of my company, ideas and the cleanliness of the whole look for the book series.

THIS IS WHY

Shatera Smith was one of the original members of my street team in 2001. She was always about her business and assisted my internship program through her company Exquisite Consulting Group. Keion McDaniels, my line brother, was someone I always looked to for advice. He was always able to give me an outside-looking- in perspective since 2002 on all of my goals included being there for me every step of the way in this process. Chris Cardwell was one of my little brothers in college. He was always there to assist with everything I needed. He's a very personable person and went on to own his own photography company in Rochester, NY. He's done multiple photo shoots for me and has always been reliable for personal and business endeavors. Khaleel Artis is my recently graduated fraternity brother. He started a logo-design company and helped create the JYM logo you see today along with digitizing my podcast design my sister, Damaris Porter, drew. The network of life grows more than you realize while in college. Khaleel crossed the same fraternity chapter in 2017 that I went into in 2003. After some tough competition, I chose his design for my personal logo. Had it not been for the network, we would not have met.

This is only a glimpse of how almost over 15 years of building a network of friends and business partners can turn into lasting relationships and with a strong network you will have people you trust to work with and be successful.

THIS IS

Communicate

I wanted to put communication alongside networking because they go hand in hand. I personally take pride in both. Communication can also be looked at as an intangible discussed earlier because it requires zero talent just like networking but these two require their own section.

I get on my network of friends and business partners all the time about this. One of the biggest mistakes we make is assuming that everyone thinks the way we think.

Communication is defined as

"the act or process of using words, sounds, signs, or behaviors to express or exchange information or to express your ideas, thoughts, feelings, etc. to someone else" ~ Merriam-Webster Dictionary

The way you interact with people consistently or even on the first meeting can determine what kind of relationship you will have with that person moving forward. You have to be able to properly communicate. In today's society, you can communicate solely by email, text, phone, and social media; you could hardly ever actually see the person. These are all ways of communication that you have to use. I personally enjoy communicating in many different ways. At the same time, some situations call for certain forms of communication. Intention and tone of voice are often communicated differently by text or email and words can also get lost in translation without being able to see the person's nonverbal communication cues.

There are some consistencies in each form of communication. I will break them down to you.

1.When you say you will do something, do it. No matter the form of communication, you are accountable for your actions. Your word is your bond. Everyone has a different sense of urgency, so if you are delegated a task or if you delegate a task to someone, be accountable and hold that person accountable to the schedule. Communicate ahead of time of the time or date given is often sufficient. Agree and hold each other to it. Things come up, we know, so just be sure to communicate any issues and plan for the adjustments. Anything can be accomplished with proper planning.

2. Be consistent with how you communicate. If you're in a leadership position, you have to be a leader and communicate with respect. You should also expect respect back. Consistency also deals with being available. You have to be able to find time to communicate, even if the text is your primary form of communication. Be available daily by text. It doesn't have to be all day. If you are only available during certain hours, make those hours known. Communicate that. Be sure to leave communication lines open to those who may need to address problems with you. The best way to communicate effectively when there is conflict is to be an active listener then respond appropriately. Go back to the chapter on intangibles if you need a reminder about how to be an active listener.

3.Do not be afraid to speak up. It's ok to be the one who voices concerns or difficulties. Whether it be in an organization, business, or personal life, be sure to be respectful in your approach and explain yourself in a way that's understandable and to the point without emotion. Be sure that you are practicing open and honest communication when doing so.

4.Communications change when you add emotion too it. I know it is hard if anyone says they communicate without emotion all the time is lying. All I suggest is to try to communicate without emotion so that you can hear opinions and with limited bias. It is very hard to do. Even an email or a text message can be seen with emotion and then responded emotionally. It is very difficult to have a productive conversation even if it's about planning an event if you don't think on a neutral mindset with very limited emotion. It's something we all have to work on.

THIS IS

5. Patience during your communications will always give them time to communicate their issues as well. I spoke earlier about being an active listener as if you are working in customer service. Remaining focused on what someone is trying to communicate will show them that you are, indeed, open to assisting with their issues. Communication lines tend to break down when there is impatience. Since you cannot control the other side, do yourself a favor and take a breath. The conversation you're involved in is important. If you are confused about what someone is requesting, then repeat back to him or her what you think they said and ask if that is correct. Often this will inspire the speaker to be more in-depth about their needs, which will help you to understand them fully. Take this advice seriously. It can really determine how you interpret a conversation.

Practicing effective communication skills helps build an effective network. Plus, you learn to become an effective leader whether the situation you face is positive or negative. If someone in your network has communicated a need or an issue to you, your main priority should be to aid him or her in repairing the problem. Following up on an issue is the only way to convince others that you have listened to them and that their problems or issues are important to you, as well. Practicing strong follow-up will also leave the impression that you are involved in the bigger picture. When people see this commitment, they will know you are helpful to include on future communications. This creates a loyal and discerning network that cultivates positive movement forward through communication. This will develop a strong mutual sense of confidence with those with whom you communicate.

THIS IS WHY

Networking Quotes from college graduates who gained success in their fields through networking and communication

"I believe networking is imperative to a person's health, wealth, and success in life. "Your network is your net worth!" The ability to connect with like-minded individuals on positive paths of interest is incredibly valuable. Networking immerses you into cultivating opportunities. Many people are capable of many things, but being afforded opportunities is key. Allow for diversified networking as doing so across multiple facets of life and industry bring about value add that one can leverage forever. I'm a living testament exemplifying how being courageous enough to network with local community, high school students and faculty, college students and faculty, industry recruiters, professional peers and champions, spiritual advisors, financial advisors, and life mentors can propel you above your circumstances and beyond your dreams."

-Derrick Taylor

THIS IS

"My Hampton network has determined the framework of my success, naturally and organically, just using the resources I had available. At the beginning of my senior year I attended the career fair at the convocation center, fresh off an investment banking internship that was only achievable with the help of my Big Brother, who had investment banking dreams and wanted me to try as well. I ran into a friend who graduated the year prior and he wanted me to apply to his firm, on the other side of the table from me at the career fair booth. He was in his first year at Accenture. Long story short, I gave him my resume, I interviewed, and I had a job offer before November of my senior year of school. I moved to DC, and 10 years later it is still one of the best decisions I ever made. Once settled in DC it was my Hampton network that got me established in the city, reconnecting with college friends, and making new friends with other alumni. When I decided I wanted to take the plunge and purchase a home, the investment was made with a Hampton realtor, and one of my longest standing friends. When I decided to pursue yoga, it was key relationships with Hampton Alum who were also native to DC that allowed me to find avenues that would have otherwise been unavailable to me. Not everyone will have the same network or the same opportunities presented to them; however, I encourage everyone to remain friendly with everyone. Be open to what everyone has to offer your life. It's insane to me that I started teaching athletes because I wasn't "skilled enough" to teach in a studio. That translated to me finding something I am REALLY good at - MOBILITY and FLEXIBILITY TRAINING - which lead me to a team, which lead me to a different team, which lead me to ALL THE TEAMS, which lead me to high schools, colleges, and professional coaches asking me for my business card and information when I walk through a gym. I have to decide how this business grows on a daily basis because nothing has been planned up to this point (I just want to teach yoga)...but KNOWING YOUR CRAFT keeps you booked and busy bruh. YOU DON'T HAVE TO SCHEME and come up with some kinda plan to promote yourself...when your results speaks for itself YOU WILL GET TALKED ABOUT. I am here for the social media thing, and I promise eventually I will be better at documentation...but you don't gotta be flexing on the gram to make money or create a brand...I am truly a testament to that. YOGA. Manifest what the fuck you are capable of, sometimes the path comes later"

-Michelle Rodgers

THIS IS WHY

Merchant's New Face Method for Success
Take Home Notes:

P.L.A.N.
Use the power of a N.E.T.W.O.R.K.
Build your network in college
People management
Take advantage of Public speaking opportunities
Communication

References:

Published by Chandler Bolt

Merriam-Webster Dictionary

THIS IS

Merchant's New Face Method for Success
9 keys to be an Effective College Student outside the classroom

1 - IT'S TIME TO SET YOUR SCHEDULE (DAILY ROUTINE)
2 - PERFECT THINGS THAT REQUIRE ZERO TALENT IT'S TIME TO
SET YOUR SCHEDULE
3 - JOIN ORGANIZATIONS
4 - BE THE X FACTOR
5 - BRAND AND INVEST IN YOURSELF
6 - CREATE YOUR N.E.T.W.O.R.K.
7 - DEVELOP YOUR NEW FACE
8 - BE A SERVANT TO THE COMMUNITY
9 - ALWAYS REMEMBER "WE PROMOTE IT"

THIS IS WHY

IX. KEY #7. DEVELOP YOUR NEW FACE

Inspirational person Pastor Mike
Train your brain
Physical Health
Working Out
Rest up
Eating Right
Yoga
Keep Fighting
Mental Health
Spiritual Health
Depression/suicide

THIS IS

Inspirational person

Rev. Michael Stewart Wortham (Pastor Mike)

Pastor Mike is a pastor, preacher, teacher, activist, and organizer. A pastor with hip-hop sensibilities, Pastor Mike has fused his love of God and hip-hop culture to reach people seeking to deepen their spirituality and fight for justice yet are skeptical of religious institutions.

Pastor Mike is a native of Fairfield, Alabama and holds a Bachelor of Science degree in Finance from Hampton University and a Masters of Divinity degree with a concentration in Race and Religion from the Candler School of Theology at Emory University. Pastor Mike served for ten years as the College and Young Adult Pastor at the Historic Ebenezer Baptist Church in Atlanta, GA, the spiritual home of the Reverend Dr. Martin Luther King, Jr.

As a student at Hampton University, Pastor Mike was very involved in campus life. He served as Senior Co-Facilitator of the Greer Dawson Wilson Student Leadership Program. He was a part of the Student Recruitment Team, NAACP, and was a mentor and volunteer at Huntington Middle School. Pastor Mike was also a part of New Face Entertainment, an organization that was responsible for many of the social activities on and off various campuses in the area.

As a minister, Pastor Mike has worked extensively with teens; college students and young adults in utilizing hip-hop culture as a teaching tool for exploring faith and spirituality. Through programs such as the Jericho Lounge, Pastor Mike blurred the lines of sacred and secular to create spaces for teens, college students, and young adults to ask tough questions about faith, religion, culture and spirituality while utilizing hip-hop elements such as emceeing and graffiti to express their thoughts. Pastor Mike has also guest lectured at colleges and universities on the intersection of faith and hip-hop.

As an activist, Pastor Mike is committed to the work of justice. In 2011, Pastor Mike assisted with efforts to help prevent the execution of then death row inmate Troy Davis by organizing a prayer vigil at Ebenezer Baptist Church held weeks prior to his execution date. In 2014, Pastor Mike founded Hymns and Hip Hop, an organization dedicated to bridging black church culture and hip-hop culture to advance the work of justice. The inaugural Hymns and Hip Hop Conference featured hip-hop pioneers Chuck D of Public Enemy and Kool

THIS IS WHY

Moe Dee, religious scholars Rev. Dr. Teresa Fry Brown and Rev. Dr. Valerie Bridgeman, and many others. Also in 2014, in the wake of the failed indictment of Darren Wilson after the death of Michael Brown and in response to multiple killings of African American men, women, boys and girls by police officers, Pastor Mike organized "Community Speaks," a community town hall forum where community members expressed their dissatisfaction with the criminal justice system in the audience of the United State Attorney General Eric Holder. In 2015, Pastor Mike helped convene African American senior pastors from across the nation for a conference to address how churches and communities can better engage in the work of social justice.

Rev. Michael Wortham, aka Pastor Mike, is a God-fearing, hip hop loving minister who is committed to motivating a generation to be carriers of love, faith, hope and justice in the world
For contacts
Social media on all platforms
@michaelswortham

Email michaelswortham@gmail.com

NETWORK
LEADERSHIP
WIN
PROFESSIONAL
ASPIRE
CHARACTER (CARE)
DISCIPLINE

THIS IS WHY

Train your Brain

You have to train your brain to create good habits while in college for your mental, physical and spiritual health. Whether you realize it or not, once you start your college journey, you are bound to come out a new person. You will have a "New Face." Everything I have mentioned throughout this book is achievable. Nothing here is so far-fetched that the average person can't go out, utilize the tools and excel past their imaginations.

Build your **NETWORK**.
Develop your **LEADERSHIP** skills.
Learn to **WIN**.
Become a **PROFESSIONAL** in your craft.
ASPIRE to do better and be better.
Build **CHARACTER** and **CARE** for others.
Build enough **DISCIPLINE** to see it through.

Physical health and appearance

Physically, I stayed in shape as much as possible while I was in college. Being in shape and physically strong is a business in itself. I always felt like I was in shape in high school. I played multiple sports, but I really didn't get into working out until I got to college. Over the years, my peers and I competed to work out. This was mainly to impress the ladies, to be honest. But we were in college. That's the point, right? But looking back at it, staying in shape and developing a routine for my physical health was important. During my freshman year, working out with Bruce at 5am, then working out with Howard in the afternoon set me up for success. We did various pull up competitions. By the time I went back home for Thanksgiving, I must have gained 10 pounds of muscle. That is only half a semester.

Sean and I worked out together all the time. Some of the ab workouts he taught me are the ones I still do to this day and I teach them to other people. Shaun and I had a workout in the pool that we called Death. It was one of the hardest workouts doing laps in the pool after two hours in the gym. When Phil got to college from Oakland, we would work out the gym for hours.

Brandon Taylor made a career out of it, becoming a professional bodybuilder after graduating.

THIS IS

Gavin McEachin worked out all the time and now does professional Cross-fit, on occasion.

Marquis Dennis is another one of my friends. We are in contact all the time about eating habits and working out.

Anwar Miles is another one of my mentees. In college, he weighed close to 300 pounds and had a health scare that changed his life forever! He was a DJ for an event in Richmond, VA and his heart suddenly started beating irregularly. Soon, his whole body froze, and he couldn't move. Because of that scare, he promised himself and God to make a change to his physical health. Presently, he's down to 165 pounds. He used to wear 4XL shirts and now he wears a small. He didn't use surgery or pills to reach his weight loss goals. He used hard work and dedication.

My advice is to make sure you take the time out to workout at least 3-5 times a week. Stay physically active for yourself and your health. I am a firm believer in 21 days to make a habit. I believe in consistency and if you want to change something you have to do it at least for 21 days in order to see change. Improve from what you did the day before. Take notes of your workout. When we worked out, we would set goals to bench press 225 pounds 10 times. The next week we would go for 11. You have to always push yourself further, or you will never know your limit.

Physical appearance plays a part as well. When I was in college, I was a businessman, leading meetings and holding leadership positions. I tried to play the part as much as possible by wearing suits, collared shirts, dress shoes and ties. When I wasn't dressed in business attire, I often wore clothes supporting my peers and their clothing lines. I knew that how I presented myself in public made a difference in how people perceived me. Being well-groomed, clean cut, and looking professional was important. Being in college is the first time you are on your own. Taking care of yourself by having a daily hygiene routine is 100% on you. It's the little things that matter. The daily routine is part of the standard you set for yourself and it can set you apart from others. Be accountable for your physical appearance and help your peers feel accountable for their appearance, as well. Wear clothes that fit and are appropriate for the occasion. For example, if you have a seminar to attend or host, it isn't appropriate to wear sweatpants and a t-shirt. If you have an 8am class, sweatpants and a t-shirt may be ok. This is the time you begin to make a name for yourself. This applies to men and women. There are different organizations that require a

THIS IS WHY

particular dress on a weekly basis. Initially, I didn't understand the purpose, but as time passed, I realized it was one of the smartest ideas. As a business major, we were required to dress in business attire on Wednesday. Acceptable business attire was a suit, shoes, button up shirt and a tie. For women, it was a suit and heels. My fraternity also had the same requirements for brothers on campus.

Get adequate rest

At 18 and 19 years old, I don't remember feeling drained. At 22-25 years old, I would pass out from stress and sleep deprivation at least once a year. I remember every October, I had five events in three days during Homecoming season in addition to having leadership roles in multiple organizations and working part time as a waiter. I remember when I was 23, I bought my first house, purchased owned three vehicles, my own business, was a full time teacher, grad student, and hosted at least one college event every week. I passed out in my house alone. Luckily when I fell out, I was next to my porch which gave me fresh air, I don't know how long I was out but I woke up in between the panels of my sliding door. Maybe the wind or air woke me up. I was stressed out and didn't know what stress is.

Getting adequate rest in college is important. You may feel like you can be up all day and night. The National Sleep Foundation recommends 7-9 hours of sleep each 24-hour period for adults. Some people need a little more or a little less. Try your best to get an average of 8 hours of sleep as often as possible even if you have to spread it out over the day. I was great at getting 2-3 hours during the day then getting an additional 4 hours at night. Rest is essential. Listen to your body.

Source:

https://www.sleepfoundation.org/press-release/national-sleep-foundation-rec-ommends-new-sleep-times

THIS IS

GET COOKING

Earlier I mentioned how I would cook for my network of friends. This was an every Sunday event. We would cook for holidays and birthdays, as well. I was never a fan of fast food, but I know in college it is easy to succumb to fast food. Take the time to learn about home economics aka cooking and managing your own home. My grandfather, Dean, played a big role in making sure I knew how to cook. He told me when I was a child that he wanted to make sure I knew how to cook so I never had to rely on someone else to eat. Learning how to cook has a number of positive effects. You will definitely develop better eating habits when you know how to cook. You save money and you don't have to eat cafeteria or fast food. Also, knowing how to cook leads to instant friends, as well. They may even be willing to buy the food for you as long as they get a plate.

Below is an article that discusses the need for home economics in the class-room even at the high school level.

https://www.dallasnews.com/opinion/commentary/2018/08/04/bring-back-home-economics-class-kids-lack-basic-life-skills

THIS IS WHY

<u>YOGA</u>

Yoga is another form of exercise that not only helps with your joints and physical movements it can help you find a sense of mindfulness and peace.

"Yoga became a part of my life because it had to, I was a few years from college and moving so fast in every area of my life. I randomly went to a yoga class, and it was the one thing that made me slow down and really clear my mind and slow my thoughts down. It also became a means of second income, which would have been something equally as easily to do in college, but it wasn't known then. Now that it is a second career for me, I see the benefits of yoga at younger ages. I primarily train athletes at the high school and college level. The decrease in the amount of injuries in the teams that I train is astounding. Simple stretches and breath techniques that can greatly change the outcome of a child college career, that is a statistic that I think needs to be taken seriously. Introducing meditation to young people ages 14-22 has also been very interesting. It is by far the favorite part of the yoga practice, they wait for asana to end so they can excitedly complete the meditation. To me, that reminds me of the origins of my personal practice, the desire to find an activity that I enjoy, that makes me slow down. I encourage everyone to at least try it. Try it for a time period, maybe 2 times a week for three months, see if once you become familiar with the language and movements if you can get into the groove of clearing you mind by connecting with your physical movements."

-Michelle Rodgers 2009 College graduate and Yoga Business owner from Michigan currently residing in DC

THIS IS

<u>Keep Fighting</u>

Even when faced with physical ailments beyond your control you have to find a way to fight through and find positives that will keep you going. Edwin Mc-Clure has been a close friend of mine for years. I have had the pleasure of meeting a majority of his family including his twin little brothers Byron and Brian. He has a story dealing with Multiple Sclerosis since college. He has been featured on the Steve Harvey Show, the CBS Early Show, local news, and myriad radio shows. By the grace of God Edwin has faced overwhelming obstacles. From terminal illness to miscarriage–he knows first-hand what it takes to persevere. Here is some information he was willing to share.

"Our sole purpose is to provide hope to a hurting world."

Coach Ed is an inspirational speaker focused on providing guidance in the areas of faith, food, and fitness. He's seen the impact improving these elements has had on his health."

– Diagnosed with Multiple Sclerosis in high school
– Had close to 10 medications fail to slow progression of disease
– Miscarriage of first child…after world saw pregnancy announcement on Steve Harvey television show
– Chronic unemployment due to recession
– Enjoyed 10 years free of Multiple Sclerosis symptoms and medications
– God blessed him with a healthy (busy) little boy and a beautiful baby girl
– Blessed to find full-time employment as well as launch business
– Now blessed with purpose to spread hope
Then in 2017. Symptoms returned

"I coach because life is hard. I believe God has shown mercy to me so I can encourage others. When going through my trials, I looked for hope and any good news anywhere I could find them. My goal is to brighten your outlook just a bit. Be it through a study, a conversation, or just knowing that someone out there knows what you are going through. We're in this fight together. If you're in the fight personally, or fighting on behalf of a loved one–we all need a teammate, and I'm here to lend a hand.

THIS IS WHY

I know firsthand the fear, shame, and rejection you are going through. I know what it's like the day after diagnosis or miscarriage. But I'm here to tell you to get up and keep going. It's not fair, and it sucks. There will probably be tears, pain, doubt, and most certainly fear…but this is our moment to prove Him. Our task is to learn His ways, and not get lost in our current storm. Just like Peter in Matt 14:29 we have to learn to look for the LORD always."

For information on Edwin and his journey visit:
www.mygreatcomeback.com
www.runmsandsicklecell.com
Contact: edmcclure89@gmail.com

Mental health

During my interview with Sianni Caballos, we talked about dealing with difficulty classes and how to make the best grades. She graduated in 2017 with a bachelor's degree in political science. In 2018, she completed her masters in nonprofit management and owner of SocialSocietyU, Inc., a lifestyle organization for high school students promoting college prep, faith and the social aspects of college. I'll get into her community organization later. During our discussion about mental health, we talked about stress and things that college students often worry about. As I mentioned intangibles earlier, you have a lot of time and freedom in college. It is up to you to use your time well. If you manage your time correctly, you will be able to pace yourself and handle more difficult classes and expectations accordingly.

I remember when I was in college, there was a class I started my sophomore year. I knew I wasn't mentally prepared to take it on. Within two weeks, I had dropped the class. I waited to try again in my junior year and passed the class with an A—. I would have definitely failed the class had I taken it my sophomore year. I knew that I didn't have the time to devote to doing well in the class that year. I had to have realistic time management goals. So, I adjusted my plan and took it at the right time, setting myself up for success.

To mentally deal with difficult classes, you have to be realistic with yourself by setting goals that you can obtain. Don't put so much on your plate that you set yourself up for failure. Pace yourself every semester. Switch it up mentally when your planning class schedule. Remember what I said? You are the expert on you. If you are a morning person, knock out your hardest classes first thing

THIS IS

in the morning. Ask around about classes and see which ones may be more difficult for you. Organize yourself between classes and organization meetings. If you are the kind of person who does best when your schedule is full, stay busy. If you are the kind of person who needs down time, plan for that. But push yourself to learn new things and make those network connections.

One goal that I recommend to everyone is to read at least 12 books per year that are not for class. I wasn't the greatest reader. I really didn't have an appreciation for books and I didn't see the point in reading stories. However, I have changed my mind about reading, but I mostly read nonfiction about topics that I am trying to learn more about. I read books to learn how to become a better writer. I read books to learn how to be a better director and producer. I read books about building wealth and real estate. The more I read, the more knowledgeable I am particular topics and it motivates me to do better in everything. Reading strengthens your mental health by keeping your brain growing with knowledge.

Dr. Byron McClure, an intern for my company as an undergrad, is now a part of the National Association of School Psychologists (NASP). Its purpose is to increase the amount of students exposed to the field of School Psychology. The primary initiative was to target undergrad students at HBCUs. It grew to all universities and high schools. By exposing and bringing awareness of school psychology to high school students, NASP increases the number of students who consider entering the field.

THIS IS WHY

In 2018 the NASP had a national conference with over 5000 psychologists from across the nation convene in Atlanta presenting at Morehouse, Spelman, and CAU.

"Overall we present to high school students and undergrads about school psychology (who we are, what we do, career paths, how we help people, the importance of mental health, etc.) to create exposure to the field and try to put a focus on attending HBCUs."~NASP

Below is the link for more information on NASP and its initiative.
https://www.nasponline.org/resources-and-publications/resources/diversity/cultural-competence/multicultural-affairs-committee/nasp-exposure-project-(nasp-ep)

THIS IS

Spiritual health on behalf of Reverend Mike Wortham

I selected Pastor Mike as an inspirational person for a number of reasons. He is a pastor, preacher, teacher, activist, and organizer and a great friend of mine. I felt like he would be the best person to speak on the importance of spiritual health.

"Dear friend, I'm praying that all is well with you and that you enjoy good health in the same way that you prosper spiritually." – 3 John 2

"Mental, physical and spiritual well-being in college can be difficult to balance. One may be able to be strong in one maybe two areas but it can be a task to find discipline in mastering all three areas. And to be honest the goal should not be to master all three areas but to be intentional about giving sufficient energy to each to help you grow into your better self as you navigate college. In this section on holistic well-being, I will offer perspective on how to foster your spiritual development while in college.

Let me begin by offering my own spiritual journey during my time in college. I began attending Hampton University in the fall of 2003. Prior to attending college, I grew up in Birmingham, Alabama and I attended church relatively every Sunday and a few days out of the week. I went to Sunday school, Bible study, choir rehearsal, step practice and would repeat this schedule week after week. I enjoyed attending church growing up because that is where I got to see many of my friends and it was definitely a highlight in my week. However, once I arrived at Hampton I was looking forward to not having to wake up in the morning, not going to church, and enjoying the luxury of sleeping on Sundays, especially after a night of partying.

My first few weeks at Hampton I took advantage of not having to get up to the sound of my mother and father waking me up to go to church. I slept in and enjoyed that extra time in the bed but as time passed I began to realize that something was missing. Although I was enjoying my time at school, I was still feeling some uneasiness. It was still taking me some time to adjust to the new setting of the Tidewater area of Virginia, which was different from my upbringing in central Alabama. I was feeling some homesickness because Hampton is ten hours away from Birmingham and I knew that I would not be

THIS IS WHY

going home until the holidays. Even though I had begun to make friends while I was there, I still felt like a connection was missing. That's when I began to realize for myself that I needed to get back to regularly attending church. Attending church at home was no problem because the place I attended had been the church for my family for four generations. I knew that I could count on my mother or father to wake me up to make sure that I got ready to attend church. Now the independence of college had gotten the best of me and now I found myself losing a piece of me. It was at this time that I decided to begin the process of finding a church to attend. Over the course of my next four years at Hampton, I worked diligently to find a community I could connect with. After two years of searching I settled upon First Baptist Church of Hampton as the place I wanted to grow spiritually.

Growing up getting to church was easy because the church I attended was pre-selected for me. I was a part of the church my family had been connected to for four generations. I didn't have to worry about the process of finding my own church. Now that I was away from home it was my responsibility to find the place, I wanted to further my spiritual development.

The first piece of advice I would suggest when looking for a spiritual home is to assess what you need spiritually. Sometimes we connect with churches, mosques or other houses of worship because they are popular or have good name recognition. Although the place may be popular and a lot of people are going there, it may not be the place that can adequately fulfill your spiritual needs. Hence, you must assess what you need spiritually before committing to a place. Assessing your spiritual needs requires self-awareness and not being afraid to look deeply within yourself to see what you need. This is also a practice should be continuous because our spiritual needs may change as we have different experiences.

After assessing your spiritual needs, the next piece of advice I would suggest is researching churches and compiling a list of places to visit. Students now have an advantage that previous generations didn't have and that is the advancement of the Internet and technology. There is more access to different religious institutions and the ability to learn more about them via their websites, apps, or videos. Based on your list of spiritual needs, you determine whether a place is worth visiting. Upon making your list begin to schedule time to visit these places and see if it is a good fit for you. The process of selecting a place takes patience because we may not find the right place on the first try. I would also

THIS IS

like to add that you should not feel pressure to go to another place, as your spiritual needs change because the goal is to grow spiritually and that could happen in more than one space.

More advice I will offer is to develop a ritual of prayer, reading, meditation and journaling. These spiritual disciplines and practices are important when working on your spiritual development. Your spiritual growth is not the sole responsibility of religious institutions, but it is an endeavor you must willingly undertake. The daily practices of prayer, reading, meditation, and journaling can undergird and sustain you while navigating the different terrains in college.

Your spiritual health is only as strong as your commitment to it. College will offer plenty of distractions that can and will take your attention from this important aspect of your life. Being intentional about your spiritual health can and will sustain you during the days when you get homesick or after many long nights of studying. The discipline of developing, growing and maintaining your spiritual health is one of the most important self-investments."

THIS IS WHY

Suicide and depression

There is no way I can release my first book without giving information on one of the most important topics in my life. Here are some steps to help save a life that I learned at the Youth Center in Queens as a teenager.

We have an obligation as a society to protect each other. Suicide and depression are issues we really don't like to discuss. As an African American male, mental health is rarely talked about because it is often frowned upon to discuss our feelings. We sometimes fear appearing emotional or "soft." I have worked to bring these topics to light ever since I was in high school. I did community service at the Jamaica Youth Mediation Corps in Jamaica, Queens. One informational seminar/play we performed was about young black male suicide and depression. Because of the potential positive impact on the community, I took the play to college with me. In addition, I put on annual events on the topic of depression and suicide; we gave out the latest statistics and educate people about the signs of suicidal and depression behavior. We did skits in which a student committed suicide because the signs were ignored. We would then repeat the skit. But, this time we showed a scenario where the signs were acknowledged and suicide was prevented. I also used my student organization, Success Without Limitations, as a platform for awareness, sponsoring annual seminars. Now, with social media, the epidemic is even worse among youth. Check out this article from the Centers for Disease Control and Prevention:

(https://www.cdc.gov/mmwr/volumes/66/wr/mm6630a6.htm)

Stress is a very real ordeal. According to the National Association of School Psychologists, stress is the way our body responds to the demands made upon it by our environment and our relationships. In teenagers that can be changing schools, moving, too much school work, divorce, pressure from home, bullying. Pretty much everything a young adult may go through can lead to good or bad stress. Bad stress over a long period of time can lead to more problems that can lead to mental and physical health issues like depression for an example.

Depression is defined as a strong mood of sadness, discouragement, and hopelessness that lasts for a long period of time (weeks, months even years)

THIS IS

The odds of adolescents suffering from clinical depression grew by 37 percent between 2005 and 2014, according to a study by Ramin Mojtabai, a professor at Johns Hopkins Bloomberg School of Public Health. Teen depression appears to be on the rise equally among urban, rural, and suburban populations. Research also shows that more dangerous behaviors, like self-harm, are increasing. Depression is the biggest risk factor for suicide in youth. Other risk factors include:

- substance abuse
- a family history of depression and mental illness
- a prior suicide attempt
- stressful life events
- access to guns
- exposure to other students who have died as a result of suicide
- self-harming behaviors such as burning or cutting
- Anxiety

Anxiety is a natural reaction to stress but when it becomes excessive it can disrupt a child's ability to function on a daily basis. There are different examples of anxiety such as obsessive compulsive disorder (OCD), Post- Traumatic Stress Disorder (PTSD, General Anxiety Disorder but I want to just focus on social phobia for the moment. Social Phobia in teens is having a strong fear of being judged by others or of being embarrassed. This affects the positive social interaction teenagers need to have at this age. In today's society, we have to address social media as well. Throughout this book I have promoted and suggested the use of social media and the internet in a positive way and I want everyone to use it for that purpose.

Social media has its positives but can also be abused by overuse and glorifying people you see. Keep in mind that social media rarely shows an individual's failures and down times. People rarely show the struggles and what it takes to get to where they are. Other people post lies. With everything I have mentioned in this book, do your research. It's nothing wrong with admiring and aspiring to be like some people on social media but make sure those people are positive influences in your life and are real.

Social media can also lead to bullying and cyberbullying.

THIS IS WHY

Sending mean-spirited messages electronically text messages and threats anonymously through phones, social media posts creating fake web pages and profiles are examples of cyberbullying according to the Substance Abuse and Mental Health Services Administration (SAMHSA). Students who are being cyber-bullied are often bullied in person as well.

Warning signs of teens dealing with stress, bullying, anxiety and depression:

- Abandoning long-time friendships for a new set of friends
- Expressing strong hostility toward family members
- Experimenting with drugs and/or alcohol
- Cutting or self destructive behavior
- Acting unusually impulsive
- Forgoing homework assignments
- Skipping school
- Sleeping excessive hours
- Loss of appetite or binge eating
- Risky behavior such as alcohol and/or drugs
- Sexual promiscuity
- Low self esteem
- thoughts/expression of suicide

Everything mentioned potentially can lead to the worst case scenario that no one wants...suicide.

The suicide rate for males aged 15–19 years increased from 12.0 to 18.1 per 100,000 population from 1975 to 1990, declined to 10.8 by 2007, and then increased 31% to 14.2 by 2015. The rate in 2015 for males was still lower than the peak rates in the mid-1980s to mid-1990s. Rates for females aged 15–19 were lower than for males aged 15–19 but followed a similar pattern during 1975–2007 (increasing from 2.9 to 3.7 from 1975 to 1990, followed by a decline from 1990 to 2007). The rates for females then doubled from 2007 to 2015 (from 2.4 to 5.1). The rate in 2015 was the highest for females for the 1975–2015 period.

According to the Johns Hopkins review in 2017:

(https://www.johnshopkinshealthreview.com/issues/fall-winter-2017/articles/the-rise-of-teen-depression)

THIS IS

The odds of adolescents suffering from clinical depression grew by 37 percent between 2005 and 2014, according to a study by Ramin Mojtabai, a professor at Johns Hopkins Bloomberg School of Public Health. The National Institute of Mental Health estimates that 3 million adolescents ages 12 to 17 have had at least one major depressive episode in the past year. Teen depression appears to be on the rise equally among urban, rural, and suburban populations. Research also shows that more dangerous behaviors, like self-harm, are increasing.

- Depression is the biggest risk factor for suicide in youth. Other risk factors include:
- substance abuse
- a family history of depression and mental illness
- a prior suicide attempt
- stressful life events
- access to guns
- exposure to other students who have died as a result of suicide
- self-harming behaviors such as burning or cutting

College is a stressful environment for most people, therefore it's especially important for parents, friends, faculty, and counselors to get involved if they suspect a student is suffering from depression. Students, themselves, are often reluctant to seek help due to social stigmas related to depression. A mental health evaluation that encompasses a student's developmental and family history, school performance, and any self-injurious behaviors should be performed to evaluate at-risk students before a treatment plan is made. The best treatments for college-aged students with depression are usually a combination of antidepressant medications and talk therapies such as cognitive behavioral therapy and interpersonal psychotherapy. Depressed students are also more likely to benefit from exercise, eating a healthy diet, and getting enough rest than many other groups. Depression can happen to any of us, especially in college. Making sure that you are eating well, sleeping enough, exercising, and managing your stress are all ways to manage your depression and risk factors.

From working with youth in the community center in Queens then doing my own seminars and plays on Suicide prevention here are some steps that we created to help prevent a potential suicide..

THIS IS WHY

Steps to preventing a potential suicide

1.No secrets-if you feel someone is showing signs of suicidal behavior, be honest and open and try your best to get the person to be honest and open. When in college and in life I feel you meet people for a reason. People come and go in your life and sometimes you wonder why. Circumstance may not just be by chance or coincidence. You may be put in someone's life to be that voice they need to hear or that ear they needed to listen.

2.Take any sign seriously. This is a very important step when you are worried that someone is thinking about suicide. If you truly care for the person and don't want to see any harm done to them make sure you take everything they say and do serious. If you see a person with wounds to their wrists that look like they tried to cut themselves, talk to them about it. Don't play around like it is a joke, seem as if you don't care when you really do inside.

3.Listen. Once the person starts to talk, listen. This step is straightforward but very important. Some people just need that person to hear what they have to say about what's going on in their life. Remember the active listening skills we've talked about. Be that person that can provide that open ear that they need to take on life longer.

4.Ask about thoughts of having suicide You don't know how many times I asked this question and it changed the whole conversation and actually HELPED! Asking someone if they are thinking about committing suicide or asking someone straight up are they going to kill himself opens the door for a conversation that will actually STOP someone from doing it. Being straight up and honest really works!

5.Don't leave a suicidal person alone Once you get to the point that you know something is wrong and that person is going to try to kill themselves, do not leave them alone. Sit talk and enjoy each other's company. Talk about things that are worth living for after listening to what is going on and what the person wants to talk about.

THIS IS

6.Urge professional help. I'm not a psychologist. I have never acted like one and neither should you unless you are one. At this point, you should make sure you insist on professional help. We discuss the topic in our community the more professional help won't be something that is frowned upon. Many insurances will cover at least some of the cost. Dr. Howard Crumpton who co founded Straight Face Entertainment with while in college is now a clinical psychologist and is someone you can reach out to be pointed in the right direction. He can be reached at drhcrumpton@gmail.com

7.From crisis to recovery below is a list of resources for those who need it. On a Personal level you don't realize how much friends and family play a role in this step.

Resources for help:

Your University/school counseling center
For information on suicidal and behavior similar to depression reach out to or contact us at www.newfacemanagement.org

www.stopcyberbullying.org
www.connectwithkids.com
www.parentingteens.com
www.kidshealth.org Nemours Kids Health
www.yellowribbon.org light for life program
www.nmha.org national mental health association

www.teenhealthcare.org free and confidential 212-423-3000 Mount Sinai adolescent health center
https://www.washingtonpost.com/news/to-your-health/wp/2018/06/07/u-s-suicide-rates-rise-sharply-across-the-country-new-report-shows/?noredirect=on&utm_term=.f7d0def42bf1

https://www.usatoday.com/story/news/politics/2018/03/19/teen-suicide-soaring-do-spotty-mental-health-and-addiction-treatment-share-blame/428148002/

ttp://therapyforblackgirls.com

THIS IS WHY

Merchant's New Face Method for Success
Take Home Notes:

Stay on top of your mental health
Workout 3-5 times a week
Monitoring your physical, mental, spiritual health can help avoid depression
Take care of your peers
Find your spiritual place
Know the steps to preventing a potential suicide

THIS IS

Merchant's New Face Method for Success
9 keys to be an Effective College Student outside the classroom

1 - IT'S TIME TO SET YOUR SCHEDULE (DAILY ROUTINE)
2 - PERFECT THINGS THAT REQUIRE ZERO TALENT IT'S TIME TO
SET YOUR SCHEDULE
3 - JOIN ORGANIZATIONS
4 - BE THE X FACTOR
5 - BRAND AND INVEST IN YOURSELF
6 - CREATE YOUR N.E.T.W.O.R.K.
7 - DEVELOP YOUR NEW FACE
8 - BE A SERVANT TO THE COMMUNITY
9 - ALWAYS REMEMBER, "WE PROMOTE IT"

THIS IS WHY

KEY #8.BE A SERVANT TO THE COMMUNITY

Sianni Caballo SocialSocietyU
Karmia Berry IAMCULTURED
Dominique Wilkins SHEChicago
Community Service
Tutoring
Shelters
Mentorship

Inspirational Organizations and Their owners

Sianni Caballo, Founder of SocialSocietyU

Sianni Caballo, after seeing the need for barriers to be broken in the lives of so many youth, set out to understand how she could eradicate the inequalities of the United States educational system were set up. She developed an invested interest in education policy and devoted herself to working with politicians on Capitol Hill.

Sianni has also launched SocialSocietyU, Inc. – where she helps first generation high school and college students prepare themselves for their next steps through workshops, College Prep Symposiums (The Gathering), and by interviewing celebrities to capture their success stories. Her events have been featured across New York City and have gathered support from BET, NBA, America's Next Top Model contestants, and more. Sianni has also reached over 500 youth across the world. To add to her successes, Sianni has also obtained her Master's Degree at Columbia University in Nonprofit Management with a concentration in Policy & Marketing. Every day she is learning how to enhance her initiatives and reach more students.

The goal of this platform is to restore dreams and to help students find their purpose. SocialSocietyU, Inc. is a college prep organization, but provides insight and resources for all routes to college.

SocialSocietyU, Inc. is a hub of college prep resources that engages and motivates high school students towards finding their purposes through faith, entertainment, college prep workshops, and by providing a taste of college culture. Every year they have their semi-annual event, "The Gathering," their college prep party and symposium. There is a live DJ, college students, university representatives, and vendors. There are celebrity panels and college prep workshops to inspire youth to garner more from their college experience. Some of SocialSocietyU, Inc past sponsors include individuals from the NBA, BET, iHeartRadio, and Wild n' Out.

https://www.socialsocietyu.com

THIS IS WHY

Karmia Berry, Founder of IAMCULTURED

Karmia Berry, Founder and Executive Director of I AM C.U.L.T.U.R.E.D. has traveled extensively visiting countries within Africa, Asia, Europe, South America, Australia, New Zealand and the Caribbean. A New York native, Karmia created an opportunity to globally enhance the learning experiences for inner-city youth at little-to-no cost to them, exposing them to world travel and encouraging them to create cultural experiences of their own. In just two year from its inception, I AM C.U.L.T.U.R.E.D. has an active roster of student traveler participants embracing their community culture and collecting passport stamps.

Karmia Berry obtained her Bachelor's of Arts in Psychology from Hampton University and her Masters of Arts in Marriage and Family Therapy from Hofstra University. She is an active member of Alpha Kappa Alpha Sorority, Incorporated.

I AM C.U.L.T.U.R.E.D., Inc. is a registered 501(c)(3) nonprofit organization, promoting self-
Empowerment and an appreciation for cultural richness and diversity by creating innovative global leaders of tomorrow to envision a life beyond their immediate communities while fulfilling personal and professional goals towards success. We aim to reduce hate and discrimination by redefining social norms through cultural immersion, education and discovery of what it means to be C. U. L. T. U. R. E. D. (Confident. Unique. Leading. Tenacious. Unstoppable. Regal. Educated. Daring) I AM C.U.L.T.U.R.E.D., utilizes mentorship, tourism, empowerment workshops and community service as tools to inspire and challenge students socially, intellectually and psychologically. Providing resources and bringing the community culture to life, we offer workshops throughout the school year in Youth Empowerment, Financial Literacy, College & Career Readiness and The Arts.

THIS IS

Why High School Students? Why Travel?

By the end of tenth grade, a student has completed their adjustment year and are now preparing for college preparatory courses, testing, as well as shaping their curriculum vitae. Traveling the world can inspire ideas, be a stress reliever and strengthen personal identity.

Cultural Series Program (is this for college students as well?)

The student traveler and their guardians participate in (5) five world travel preparatory workshops, prior to the students' departure. The workshops are mandatory and are designed to build engagement between the student traveler, IAC Ambassadors and chaperone. The student traveler is responsible for completing assignments and journaling throughout this globally enhanced learning experience.

- IAC Summer Cultural Series Program Benefits
- Obtain a passport
- School-based and community fundraising and service opportunities
- Five empowerment & world travel preparatory workshops
- Week-long excursion to another country
- College prep and mentorship program
- Small travel groups
- College scholarship
- Once-in-a-lifetime memories with lifelong friends
- Community Culture

https://www.iamcultured.org

THIS IS WHY

Dominique Wilkins, Co founder of SHEChicago

Since leaving Hampton, Dominique Wilkins has worked 8 years in Finance, Business to Business sales, and as a Leading Consultant in the Beauty Industry before embarking upon her journey in education in 2015. Domonique's love for the beauty industry and entrepreneurial spirit began as a young girl, and has allowed her to become a beauty influencer whose impact is nationwide. Holding strong to the motto that "when you look good, you feel good," she has been able to help women enhance their public images and build healthy self-esteem through proper self-care.

As a mother of two beautiful daughters, Makeup Artist, and Music Educator on the Southside of Chicago, Dominique has been blessed with a heart for people. That heart extends to the work that she does as a co-founder of SHE. Helping young women to channel their strength, humility and be empowered through a focus on Health and Beauty is a direct reflection of the calling on her life, and she is eternally grateful for the opportunity to serve.

SHE began as a conversation between Dominicca Troi Washington and Dominique Natasha, two teachers at a high school in Chicago's South Shore Community, while on a summer road trip to Detroit. The pair shared their life stories with one another, and spoke about their passion for urban youth, particularly young women.

While discussing the possibility of starting a young women's club for their school, both agreed that the name "young women's club" did not fully embody what they wanted to give to the girls they worked with. During their brainstorming session, Dominique turned to Dominicca and said "What about SHE?" The name was a perfect fit, but it was important to both women that it had meaning as well, so the discussion continued. Dominicca suggested the name be an acronym which prompted discussion around what defines a whole woman, better yet, a whole human. It didn't take long for the two to agree that SHE simply means to be Strong. Humble. and Empowered. Excited about what was to come, Dominicca committed herself to developing a strand focused on building the Social and Self Awareness of female youth, while Domonique committed to developing a strand focused on building the image and self-esteem of female youth through Health and Beauty.

THIS IS

Upon the start of the school year, as the program began to gain momentum, Dominicca realized that SHE was missing a key component. The curriculum needed a focus area that would culminate the girls' experiences with both strands, and allow them to put what they learn into practice. After some discussion around the need for a well-rounded curriculum, both agreed that a College and Career Readiness section was needed, and Marrissia Jones, a fellow educator at their school, seemed like an ideal candidate to head this section. The idea was proposed to Marrissia and she agreed to join the team by developing and directing the third and final strand of SHE. SHE's pilot program launched in September 2017, accepting 44 bright and brilliant young ladies with an overall GPA of 3.7.

http://www.shechicago.org

THIS IS WHY

<u>Community Service</u>

Community service is defined as voluntary work intended for the common good usually done as part of an organized scheme. Many dictionaries also define community service as a way people may avoid jail time when facing punishment for a crime. That is NOT what I mean when I talk about community service. Community service is what society needs; it's how people positively give back to others in need. There are a number of ways to provide community service. Being involved in community service projects can help you decide what you actually want to do for a living.

Sometimes community service can be used to fine-tune your skills for your career. Chris Queen was able to take his experience as my intern in 2005 doing well over the required amount of community service to satisfy is internship by getting experience in his craft. During his sophomore year in college, he performed over forty hours of community service during the second semester providing video and DVD production support for various campus events. He recorded dance competitions, Greek probates, step shows fashion shows, and pageants for the various organizations. He filmed the events, then he transferred the footage to his PC, edited them. burned them to DVDs, designed DVD covers and cases, and assembled the packaging. He did this all as a community service for the various organizations earning him the community service credit and internship needed. Now he owns his own website company Chris Queen Consulting www.chrisqueen.com where does website design and consultations.
It is important to find ways to give back as we increase our own knowledge and experience. Being that encouraging presence in a community is imperative. Remember that creating that positive residual impact can help younger students develop their own plans and reach their goals as they come up behind you.

When I was in college, I knew I wanted to do something for the community. I always said I wanted to build an after-school program for high school kids, focused on both academic and sports activities. When I was initiated into the Gamma Iota chapter of Alpha Phi Alpha Fraternity, Inc. and was doing community service with the Go To High School Go To College Initiative I thought maybe this is it. My company and my fraternity sponsored families for the holidays who couldn't afford a Thanksgiving or Christmas dinner. When I started SWL at ODU while in grad school, I thought maybe that was what I was looking for. When I turned New Face into an actual business with intern-

THIS IS

ships and scholarships, I knew I was on the right track. I began to feel it was how I was supposed to change the world. As a high school teacher, I thought I had found my calling. I felt proud to get up every day and go to work. The experiences I've had where I was able to give back and impact change just felt right: when I lived in Panama for three months, as a father, as a coach. Even now creating this publication and my documentary to give to the community so they can do better than my peers and I, gives me joy and a sense of accomplishment. Maybe that's the community service I've been looking for. I just know I'm here to make a difference and change the world somehow.

In 2004, through my event planning company New Face Entertainment, I put a name to the various community service ventures done as a company called Success Without Limitations. An assortment of college students applied and received financial scholarships. Student organizations such as Fraternities and Sororities receive monetary donations in the thousands. Seminars covering suicide prevention and depression were held in the name of SWL. Campus beautification projects were also executed like the repaving of basketball courts on college campuses. SWL (Success Without Limitations) is still active to this day with over 200 members. The campus SWL still has the same mission of giving back to the community through service.

We as a company sponsored a youth basketball team in Newport News, Virginia. College students sponsored a youth basketball team, found a gym for students and ran practices. Every week at our Tuesday meetings we would report the status on the team. We always found a way through our platform success without limitations to give back to the community and made it fun for the students involved. It is much easier to wake up and do things you want and love to do than it is to do things you feel like you HAVE to do. Just imagine how it feels to be able to give kids the opportunity to be on a basketball team or the feeling that comes from giving a family a proper thanksgiving. It's the best feeling in the world.

I wanted to create something that had a lasting effect past the time created it. Success without limitations was that for me.

THIS IS WHY

For Sianni Caballo, Karmia Berry, and Dominique Wilkins, it was SocialSocietyU, IAmCultured, and SHEChicago, respectively. We were able to have an impact on the community that will permanently change the lives of our youth. These are the goals you want to set. Even if you don't want to create a new organization, you can be a part of organizations like these and impact a student's life to make them better. That's the purpose: to bring our community to a rise in your own way.

Tutoring was big for me, as well. My fraternity, the Gamma Iota chapter of Alpha Phi Alpha Fraternity, Inc. would go to an elementary school and tutor students weekly. After the tutoring session was completed, we would go and play sports and other games with them. There are plenty of tutoring programs you can be a part of on campus and in communities across the country.

Nikki Walker, my former personal assistant, once worked in a shelter for survivors of domestic violence. Together, we would host an annual food and clothing drive where we collected donations of canned goods and lightly used coats and took them to a women's shelter in the Hampton Roads area. I always made a point to do what I could as a business owner. But I also relied on the community to make money to be able to give back to those in need.

"Great leadership isn't about control. It's about empowering people."

-Unknown

THIS IS

Be a Mentor

A mentor is defined as a wise and trusted counselor or teacher or as an influential senior sponsor or supporter. Serving as a mentor falls under community service, but it means so much more. Being a mentor means you may be like a big brother or sister to someone who needs extra support in their lives. Some mentors come to mean more to people than actual family. Imagine being able to guide someone through the most critical points in their lives as college students entering a new environment for the first time. Everything you learned up until this point can steer a person into the right direction so they will be a step ahead. Utilizing your personal experiences along with this book will make the experience of being a mentor that much easier and more fulfilling. If you're reading this as an incoming freshman or as a high school senior, be sure to find someone you have like interests with and someone you can look up to point you in the right direction. I have little brothers and sisters that I have mentored for over 15 years and, to this day, I still offer advice; we learn from each other, in fact. A mentorship is when you mentor a person or group of people over a period of time. You never know how a relationship like being a mentor can affect someone or affect you until it happens.

One example of a mentor is "This is why you go to college" documentary participant, Matthew White who works for the university where he attended school. Matt has been a great mentor for students coming after him. As an educator and an administrator, he makes a huge difference in the lives of others by just talking and allowing them to learn from his past experiences. Matt is the director of University relations and serves as Hampton University's spokesperson. He is the lead of administrative announcements, breaking news, and press queries. He may not realize it, but to see an alumnus work for the same school he graduated from means a lot to students, especially those who develop a love for the university and are interested in being in education themselves.

Many of the organization that I talked about in the "Join organizations" chapter include some mentoring component. It is common for student leadership programs, the Greek organizations, and success without limitations to have mentoring or leadership requirements. They are all deeply vested in mentorship.

When you Invest in each other you never know the lasting effect that has on you and the people involved. Previously I mentioned meeting the McClure family starting with the older brother Edwin in 2003-2004 and then twins Byron and Brian McClure when they visited Hampton University while on a college tour. I immediately took Edwin and, later Brian, under my wing when they enrolled at Hampton. Edwin was a member of my company and received opportunities to promote his clothing company. I got him the opportunity to design the outfits for the 2005 probate show of the Gamma Iota Chapter of Alpha Phi Alpha, Fraternity, Inc. Brian McClure, at one point, almost failed out of school and was put on academic probation but we were able to turn it around. He still thanks me almost 15 years later for keeping him on task in undergrad as his mentor. They both are my Fraternity brothers becoming Alphas in 2007 and both are doctors. Bryon has as doctorate degree from Indiana University of Pennsylvania and is a nationally certified school psychologist. Brian received his doctorate from the University of Memphis in US and African American History and serves as the director of policy and legislative affairs in DC under the Office of Ward 5 council member Kenyan McDuffie. Once again you never know how much of influence you can have on people as a mentor. Do your part and change lives for the better.

"Each one teach one"

THIS IS

Merchant's New Face Method for Success
9 keys to be an Effective College Student outside the classroom

1 - IT'S TIME TO SET YOUR SCHEDULE (DAILY ROUTINE)
2 - PERFECT THINGS THAT REQUIRE ZERO TALENT IT'S TIME TO
SET YOUR SCHEDULE
3 - JOIN ORGANIZATIONS
4 - BE THE X FACTOR
5 - BRAND AND INVEST IN YOURSELF
6 - CREATE YOUR N.E.T.W.O.R.K.
7 - DEVELOP YOUR NEW FACE
8 - BE A SERVANT TO THE COMMUNITY
9 - ALWAYS REMEMBER, "WE PROMOTE IT"

THIS IS WHY

KEY #9. ALWAYS REMEMBER, "WE PROMOTE IT"

Inspirational Person Angel Rich
Exploration
Travel
RESPONSIBLE DRINKING
WE Promote it
Safer sexual activity

THIS IS

Inspirational person
Angel Rich

Creating an algorithm for the stock market to win Goldman Sachs Portfolio Challenge, selling her first marketing plan to Prudential, becoming a founding employee of FINRA, authoring the first ever African American Financial Experience study, inventing the top financial literacy product in the world, and being named the "Next Steve Jobs" by Forbes – all by age 30, Angel Rich has earned the title "Wealth Pioneer."

In 2009, Angel became a Global Market Research Analyst for Prudential Financial. While there, she conducted over 70 financial behavior studies including the Obama's Veterans Initiative. During her final year at Prudential, she helped the company's Annuities division grow from #16 in Service to #4, helping the company save $6 billion.

After leaving, Angel founded The Wealth Factory with a mission to provide equal access to financial literacy across the world. Today her company designs WealthyLife financial literacy education technology games. The online games are supported by financial curriculum, programming and activities, walking people from birth to retirement in 12 subjects. The first game released is titled CreditStacker. This match-three game, like Candy Crush, allows users to swap colored pieces representing the 5 major credit types, to pay off debt, achieve a high credit score, and learn from the multiple-choice questions. It has been named the best financial literacy product in the country by The White House, Department of Education, and JP Morgan Chase.

In August 2017, the company launched the full product version of CreditStacker, exceeding 200,000 downloads in 60 countries in 21 languages in two weeks. Google named it one of the Top 10 Apps in the world of 2017 and 2018. It's the #1 most downloaded education app in 14 countries; it's among the top 5 in 40 countries.

The Wealth Factory's goal is to transform financial marketing to financial education while reducing poverty, increasing financially savvy citizens, raising financial product ownership and building better financial ecosystems. In early 2017, Angel also released her first book – The History of the Black Dollar – with a foreword written by Dr. Maya Rockeymoore. The book takes readers on an economic journey through history to depict the major milestones, historic figures and upcoming leaders.

Later that year, she was honored to be named Hamptonian of the Year and help found the Hampton University Entrepreneurship and Innovation Institute. She is also a proud member of the 2016 HBCU 30 Under 30, Hampton 40 Under 40 and Google Top 30 Black Female Founders.

In 2018, the MIPAD named her one of the Top 100 Most Influential People in the African Diaspora and one of four Icons, establishing a partnership to offer financial literacy to the African Diaspora. Later that year, she was appointed Commissioner of Financial Literacy by the Mayor of DC.

THIS IS

Exploration

Even conservative parents will tell you that when you go to college, it is the time for you to explore and find yourself, but they may not tell you what that means. This chapter will give you some direction about what it means to "be free" and "find yourself." It provides some tips about what exploration might mean and how young people can explore safely without sacrificing fun.

Parents, counselors, and mentors tend not to talk about the "real" incidents that happen when you get to college. Most people don't want to talk about the underage drinking, parties, road trips and sex that takes place in college. The truth of the matter is that for many college students, this is their first taste of freedom, with no penalty for coming home late or staying out all night. This is a time to try new things that may not have been acceptable when you were under the watchful eye of your parents. My objective in this chapter is to provide you with some Dos and Don'ts to related to having fun but avoiding unwanted trouble such as expulsion from college, a criminal record, or even an unplanned child.

Travel

One of the great things about college is you will meet people from places you have never been. You will come across people who may or may not look just like you but you have so many things in common that it's hard to believe you are just meeting for the first time. You may have the opportunity to travel to meet your new friends' families during holidays and academic breaks. Do it! This is your new network, your new extended family. Use spring break and summer periods to travel with your friends to cities and countries you have never been to. Feed off of each other's energy and experiences and make new ones as young adults. If you are from Florida and have a dorm mate who is from New York, you could spend a whole year together, become close friends, and start calling each other's parents "mom and dad." A year can feel like a decade of friendship. While you're visiting, see for yourself what a winter in New York City is like; New York is much bigger than times square. If you're from New York, visit your friend from the South and see what southern hospitality is really like. Go to Florida and see palm trees and warm weather in December.

THIS IS WHY

One of the first things I did after I completed my first year of college was to spend a month in Oakland, California with one of my best friends, Howard Crumpton. It was my first visit to the West Coast, and I took full advantage of it. Thanks to Howard, I was able to experience as much of California as I could. I noticed that San Francisco was one of the most liberal "free" cities I have ever seen to this day. I saw Berkeley in Northern California. I was able to spend time in Oakland. I witnessed the culture and the vast differences between the East and the West and the differences between San Francisco and Oakland. We drove from Oakland to Los Angeles then down to San Diego. I didn't realize until then that Oakland is almost 6 hours away from LA by car. I thought it would be more like going from Queens to Brooklyn which is thirty minutes at the most. Howard taught me how to drive a stick shift on that trip to southern California. I had never seen desert mountains in person before. Coming from New York, I heard about "a house on a hill" and I immediately thought it referred to a mansion in a wealthy area. I noticed very quickly in both northern and southern California that having a house on a hill does not mean that at all. It can be a modest house on a hill with a nice view. The way of living was so different in comparison to what I was used to. There were four-lane highways, minimal public transportation, palm trees, and temperate climates.

During my time in college, I traveled to various cities within the United States: Chicago, DC, Charlotte, Atlanta, Miami, Dayton. I went on a road trip after road trip. If there was an event that was driving distance away, I was there even if it was multiple states away. I had traveled to Jamaica as a part of a senior trip, but that was the only time I had gone out of the country in college. As I said before, this book is designed to educate you to learn from what my network and I did and to learn what we did NOT do. I strongly suggest you travel to the various cities where your peers live. But you should also travel together to various countries as well. Educate yourself and explore other cultures.

I mentioned IAMCULTURED when I spoke about community service. Two close friends of mine Karmia Berry & Shatera Smith use IAMCULTURED to bring the idea of travel to life by giving young people an opportunity even before college to travel to different countries and experience cultures.

I read a great article from 2016 written by a college student named Evelyn Atieno. Ms Atieno gave tips for traveling to different parts of the world as a "broke" college student. She went over key items like when and where to go, how to find deals, saving money on food, taking advantage of free tours, etc.

THIS IS

Here's a link to the article in case you find it as helpful as I did in thinking of ways to stretch your travel budget.

https://www.huffpost.com/entry/8-ways-to-travel-as-a-bro_b_9717512

I strongly suggest studying abroad in college and if you don't have a minor take a minor in a 2nd language and take a semester abroad. You will thank me later.

Responsible drinking

The reality is many college students have tried drinking before coming to college. The legal drinking age is twenty-one so any drinking prior to that age you are taking a risk of making irresponsible decisions that will lead to you not being able to achieve your goals while in college. Don't do things to jeopardize your goals. I have given you the tools in this book that will be altered and won't be done to perfection of you decide to drink especially illegally under the age of twenty-one. It took me a while to realize it but trust me when I tell you, its ok to party without having to drinking and you will still have a great time.

Drinking while in college is one of those topics that isn't discussed enough before a young adult moves away from his parents. In reality, plenty of high school students have had alcoholic drinks at the very least at their prom or at a graduation party. Drinking under the age of twenty-one is illegal. I don't condone underage drinking at all, but I've been to college and know what takes place. As an adult in my 30's, I have a responsibility to be realistic with our young adults and properly prepare them for all aspects of life. Young adults will eventually be on their own and need to make a decision on their own.... It's our job to give them the proper tools to at least know what can happen and what the result of their actions may be. We owe it to them to share our past experiences and the experiences of our friends.

You may hear a campus referred to as a "dry" campus meaning they don't allow alcohol to be served at on-campus events. It may also mean that alcohol is not permitted on campus at all regardless of age. A "wet" campus may allow alcohol to be served at events such as football games and parties that are designated for students who are 21 and older. All must still abide by the laws. That

THIS IS WHY

means that there are no campuses, wet or dry, that allow people who are under 21 to drink alcohol. It's also illegal to provide alcohol to people under 21.

Obviously, the majority of college students do not turn 21 until about mid-way in their junior year. Anyone with common sense knows that alcohol is available in college is easier to get than that calculus 101 syllabus. This is where the responsibility and accountability come into play. As adults who have teenagers turning into young adults, it's our responsibility to teach them real life scenarios and to be accountable for themselves and others.

From personal experience, I can say I drank all throughout college. I wasn't 21 until March my junior year. Some of my friends in college never drank, not even occasionally. They chose to abstain. Was I the most responsible? Absolutely not. As I said earlier, this is one of those opportunities to learn from my peers and me. Did I ever end up in the hospital due to alcohol poisoning? NO. Were there times I drank too much and ended up passed out on the floor somewhere? YES. Did I have friends who ended up in the hospital? Yes. Did we always have people watching out for each other? Yes. Accountability is very important. Drinking alcohol can change the whole dynamic of the day especially in college. When done in moderation after you turn twenty-one is not a terrible thing but it's very rare that college students think with the mind of moderation or pacing. That is why it is very important to have friends, male and female, who are accountable for each other.

Never ever under any circumstances should you drink and get behind the wheel and drive. It's not worth your life, your friends' lives or the lives of anyone who may be on the road. There are too many other options for transportation that driving under the influence should not even be an option. I have friends who have lost licenses, totaled cars, and lost lives due to driving after having very little alcohol. Not to mention, if you get pulled over, you are liable to get arrested, go to jail, and get kicked out of college. I have heard stories of students driving on the wrong side of the highway because they got intoxicated at a party. I have heard stories of students who didn't make it home safely, students getting arrested for public intoxication and DWIs. As a young adult, you won't know your limit until you hit that limit. By then, it may be too late.

THIS IS

I say all of that to tell you the real consequences of drinking and driving. I can't say it enough… Always have a designated driver to get you to and from events. Be safe and responsible. Otherwise, you poor choices may have a negative impact on the rest of your life.

Even if you aren't driving, there is a responsibility that comes with drinking. 1. You have to know yourself, and listen to your friends who know you, too. If you know that when you take more than three shots you have trouble walking, maybe you might want to stop at two. If your friends are telling you to stop, stop. You can have a great time drinking at a party. You can have a great party without drinking. You can have a great time just hanging out with friends..
Here is some information about drinking on campuses:

Binge Drinking Statistics according to

https://www.responsibility.org/college-binge-drinking-statistics/

"According to the 2016 Monitoring the Future Study, 81% of college students have tried alcohol at least once in their lifetime and 67% report they have been drunk. More important, perhaps, is the occurrence of binge drinking — 32% of college students report binge drinking (having consumed five or more drinks in a row at least once in the two-weeks prior to completing the survey).

Trends in alcohol consumption continue to reflect long-term declines among college students. Since 1991, lifetime consumption among college students has declined 13% proportionately, while annual consumption and monthly consumption are down 11% and 15%, respectively. Additionally, the overall trend in binge drinking among college students continues to show a decline, decreasing 24 percent proportionally since 1991 (from 43% to 32%) and 21 percentage points over the past decade. From 2015 to 2016 there were no measurable changes in the reported levels of consumption at all prevalence rates measured by the study. Nevertheless, college students continued to self-report slightly higher annual, 30-day, and binge drinking rate of alcohol consumption than their non-college age peers. (Source: University of Michigan, Monitoring the Future, 1975-2016: Volume II, College Students and Adults Ages 19-50, 2017)

THIS IS WHY

The Monitoring the Future Study (2005-2016 combined data) revealed during the two weeks prior to the survey about one in eight (12%) college students reported they have consumed 10 or more drinks in a row at least once, including one in twenty-five (4%) who reported consuming 15 or more drinks in a row. (Source: University of Michigan, Monitoring the Future, 1975 2016: Volume II, College Students and Adults Ages 19-50, 2017) "

So, that article was about the numbers of college students who may be drinking. Here is a portion of an article about some of the risks that go along with drinking.
https://www.alcoholrehabguide.org/resources/college-alcohol-abuse/

"Drinking can increase a person's risk of injury, ranging from minor cuts to broken bones or concussions. The higher someone's blood alcohol content (BAC) level, the greater the chance of getting injured. Each year, close to 600,000 college students unintentionally injure themselves due to heavy drinking. Injuries can involve bruising, fractures, muscle sprains and other similar issues. For those who struggle with depression or anxiety, alcohol consumption can cause life-threatening effects. Students who face extreme mental instabilities are most at risk of attempting to commit suicide or other acts of self-harm. Alcohol can significantly alter a person's mind, which can make them act irrationally.

Alcohol is known to lower a person's inhibitions and therefore, makes them more vulnerable to physical or sexual assault. Close to 700,000 students between the ages of 18 and 24 are assaulted by a student who had been drinking prior to the offense."

Another serious crime linked closely to alcohol use is sexual assault. All too often, perpetrators prey on victims who have been drinking. Victims are some-times too incoherent to fight back or pass out before knowing what happened. Sexual assault can have a lasting effect on someone emotionally and physically, including getting a sexually transmitted disease (STD), having an unwanted pregnancy, or causing lasting psychological damage.

When someone is under the influence of alcohol, their actions may be entirely different from how they would normally behave. The may commit, no matter how minor it may be, that they wouldn't have committed if they were sober.

THIS IS

Highly intoxicated college students usually partake in vandalism, property damage, driving under the influence, and other criminal activities.

Sometimes though, alcohol-related crimes can be extremely serious and put other people in danger. Harmful criminal activities involve battery, kidnapping, and homicide. College students who commit crimes while intoxicated can face legal punishments such as fines, probation, suspended licenses, and jail time.

The effects of heavy drinking do not always happen immediately. It may take months or even years for some effects to occur. Nearly 150,000 college students develop some type of alcohol-related health problem every year. This may include liver damage, high blood pressure, inflammation of the pancreas and other health complications.

College students who participate in frequent drinking activities are also more likely to develop a dependency on alcohol later in life. Although alcoholism typically results from years of drinking, it can also happen during periods of heavy and frequent drinking during college. Bad drinking habits in college can evolve into other issues, like alcoholism, in the future."

www.responsibility.org is a website that give different resources to avoid drunk driving, underage drinking, drinking responsibly and help centers across the country

We Promote it !

As someone who made thousands of dollars for years throwing weekly parties for college students as a college student, I am the first to tell you to go out and have a great time, but be responsible. One of the biggest messages we promoted consistently was a phrase called "We promote IT.' I produced shirts, we talked about it constantly, and provided safe ways to do IT. The IT that we were referring to is safe sexual activity: safe sex. That can mean a number of things, not just about the actual activity. Make sure you don't drink to the point that you cannot make a safe sound decision. Make sure you surround yourself with friends you can trust. Always have and use condoms; there are male and female condom options. Sexually transmitted infections and diseases and pregnancy are not issues you want to deal with while in college. Neither is it something people plan for no matter what they say after the fact, and no matter

THIS IS WHY

how maturely it is handled afterward. No one plans to have a child in college, and no one intentionally contracts a sexually transmitted disease. As a college student, you are going to want to enjoy yourself, and have a great time being away from home. There is a safe way to do so without putting yourself in danger and without making a decision you may end up regretting later.

I am a strong advocate for safe sex but you have to be responsible. The most responsible way to do that is to practice abstaining from sex. Peer pressure is a serious thing, especially in college. I am using the platform to let you know that you will be making a lot of the decisions on your own so be aware there are serious consequences for your decisions and actions. Don't allow anyone pressure you to do anything you don't want to do. Be an independent smart thinker.

Sex is one of those things that can be hard for people to talk about, yet everyone assumes that everyone else knows what they are doing. Many parents don't feel comfortable talking to their kids about it, and friends talk about sex like everyone is a professional. My event planning company, New Face Entertainment, threw an annual event called the safe sex party where we would give out free condoms along with the statistics in the area for HIV and Sexually Transmitted Diseases. As college students throwing parties for college students, we would have literally over 1,000 people every week partying, so we tried our best to take advantage of the "platform" we had in a number of different ways. One goal was to promote safe sexual activity knowing that by the end of the night many students wanted to "get closer" with their peers. In today's society, it is even more important to ensure that whatever sexual activity takes place is consensual. By consensual I mean that all those involved have given enthusiastic consent for all sexual action to take place. Enthusiastic consent means that if someone is too drunk, passed out, or nervous to say yes, the answer is a no. Yes means yes. This is true for everyone, men and women. If you are unsure or your partner is not giving you an enthusiastic yes, just don't do it. Remember to abstain is the best form of safe sex.

You are in college to have fun, but you must strike a balance. I cannot tell you how many people say they dropped out or failed out of school because they partied too hard or made the wrong decisions. You can party, run multiple organizations, have a 3.0 GPA, and a part time job. I am not telling you because I believe it. I am telling you because I did it. I want you to be better than me. I set the standard, and I want everyone reading this book to be inspired and motivated to know you can do it better than I did.

Practice Safer Sex

The Well Project is a non-profit organization whose mission is to change the course of the HIV/AIDS pandemic through a unique and comprehensive focus on women and girls. They are a recognized leader in the fight against HIV, revolutionizing the availability and accessibility of meaningful and relevant information designed specifically for women and girls living with HIV. On their site, they have information on sex education and safe sex practices. Here is just a portion of the information I found. Please go and view the site when you have time:

"Safer sex can be fun, exciting, and very pleasurable. It can make your sex more relaxed and satisfying, by decreasing your worry about getting or spreading sexually transmitted infections or diseases (STIs or STDs). It is also a great chance to add variety to your sex life, and to build trust and intimacy with your partner(s), by talking about each other's desires.

Some health conditions, which may become serious without treatment, can be passed from one person to another through sex. Safer sex is sex that reduces the chances of spreading or getting STIs. It involves certain actions (e.g., using a condom, taking HIV drugs) that prevent person-to-person sharing of bodily fluids that are able to spread STDs. Choosing to have safer sex shows that you care about the pleasure and health of yourself and your sexual partner(s).

For people living with HIV, safer sex is important because it can prevent infection with other STDs that can weaken the immune system. If both people are living with HIV, safer sex can also reduce the chances of getting another strain of HIV that is resistant to the HIV drugs you are taking. Taking HIV drugs is also a part of safer sex for people living with HIV. When a person's viral load has reached undetectable levels (not enough HIV in their bloodstream for a test to measure), they cannot transmit HIV to anyone through sex."

https://www.thewellproject.org

THIS IS WHY

III - AFTER COLLEGE APPLY WHAT YOU LEARNED

Building character while creating your adult self

The WHY

THIS IS WHY

Inspirational People

Chris Roy

Chris Roy is a digital 1st marketing mind that has created and executed groundbreaking campaigns that have positioned brands like REVOLT TV into the forefront of conversation amongst millennial audiences.

His charismatic personality and business savvy launched his company, The Lifestyle Agency, into the spotlight as one of LA hottest new entertainment and creative groups. The Lifestyle Agency is a full service creative agency that specializes in experiential marketing and concierge services. Passion and consistency is what drives our brand. He prides himself on building and maintaining relationships in every major market in the Country. With over 10 years of experience working with the nation's top entertainers, venues, and brands, we create memories that will last a lifetime.

Our groundbreaking campaigns and entertainment franchises set a standard of excellence in the LA Market. Chris' seamless transition from the boardroom to the forefront of LA's nightlife scene is something really unique. The duality in his personality makes for an interesting conversation starter at all times.

His relentless work ethic and faith have kept him grounded in a fast moving scene that can exaggerate your highs and lows. The foundation of Chris' work ethic has always been rooted in his mother's consistency and drive. Born in Washington DC and raised in Chesapeake, Virginia hard work, keeping family first, and staying on top of education are principles that his mother instilled in him from a young age that have paid off in his success today.

Chris had a very well-rounded college experience, attending two of the top HBCUs in the nation. He developed his business acumen and relentless drive for excellence at Morehouse, and his ability to build community and love for curating culture form Hampton. Chris graduated from Hampton with a business marketing degree in 2008. The combination of these unique experiences and valuable lessons along the way have positioned him to be very unique in his arena.

THIS IS

Chris's agency is expanding into real estate and large scale event production. Faith, vision, and consistency have driven him to manifest his childhood dreams now he has shifted his focus to build a legacy for generations to come.

Chris Roy
Founder & CEO
www.TheLifestyle.Co
chris@thelifestyle.co

THIS IS WHY

Shatera Smith

Shatera Smith is a Human Resources professional with eleven years of experience. She is a living example of striving and grinding to make an impact in the world by sharing her talents, wisdom, and unselfishness. She is the Founder and CEO of Exquisite Consulting Group, LLC, a company that offers HR services for the creation of comfortable, yet productive work atmospheres to individuals and small businesses. The company also offers College Preparation consulting to organizations or to students looking to pursue higher education.

She is the Employee Relationship Generalist for the City of East Orange, where she partners with Directors, Supervisors/Managers, and staff within the agency to advise employees on the proper procedures, and/or resolutions, in handling personnel matters and issues to foster a positive environment. She works closely with management to determine staffing requirements, identifies and recommends potential candidates for departments, counsel managers on supervisory skills to increase communications, clarify expectations, and improve performance. She assists with development and implementation of personnel policies and procedures, HR special projects, processes, and programs. She is also the Marketing manager for Slantress Magazine, where she is responsible for building relationships, promoting events, and speaking on behalf of the company.

She is the founder of P. L. O. T. (Prolific Leaders of Tomorrow), a College/ Career readiness program through her company (Exquisite Consulting Group, LLC), designed to mentor students in 10th — 12th grade with life goals. The program focuses on helping students develop a specific career path or plan. It provides several ways students can use to develop a plan, supported by college and career readiness resources and one on one consulting. Students will understand and be able to articulate the match between their personal interests/goals and their preparation plan for college/careers.

With God as her foundation, Shatera has a positive and bright outlook. Her passion for helping others and making a difference in the lives of others positions her to bring changes to the community. She holds seats on several organizations including:

THIS IS

- The Steering Committee for Essex County Young Democrats
- Director of Community Relations for I AM CULTURED, Inc – 501(c)(3) non-profit organization that utilizes travel, mentorship and community service as tools to inspire and challenge high school students socially, intellectually and psychologically,
- Treasurer for former Hudson County Freeholder Gerard Balmir, JR,
- NY/NJ Ambassador for Project Hygiene, 501(c)(3) non-profit organization established to support underprivileged youth, ages 10-18 by promoting health and wellness while denouncing bullying.

She sits on two ministries within her church. She is the Coordinator for The City of East Orange Music, Arts, and Cultures Festival, managing the Entertainment and Logistics of festival.

Contact Shatera for more information on her various ventures:
shaterasmith@exquisiteconsultingroup.com

THIS IS WHY

THE WHY
Final chapter - Learn from us

THIS IS

Success isn't always a straight path

According to www.socialsocietyu.com (See servant to the community section), 20% of students who drop out do so because they feel "school simply wasn't relevant to their lives." If that's how you feel while in college at any point, you may be doing something wrong. I agree that not all classes are equally relevant at all times. Some things you learn, you may never use again. But if you learn anything from this book, I want it to be that you're not in college just to go to class. That diploma is supposed to be mean so much more than a degree is the classroom. The diploma represents the network you built and the relationships you nurtured, as well as your own maturity, independence, and growth. Your experiences going to college and graduating give you the credibility you need to prove you completed this on your own and didn't quit. It shows that you can do something on your own, set a goal and complete that goal. What you learn in college outside the classroom may be more influential in your life and shape you into the person into the person you will become. It takes the four+ years of personal growth inside and outside the classroom to fully appreciate all the benefits of college.

Never give up your goals. Finish what you started. No one goes to college planning not to graduate. We all know things happen. We can't control every-thing that takes place in our lives. We can do our best to control what we can control but circumstances happen beyond our control that change and delay our path. It is a myth that success is straight line. Success is a consistent movement forward. When it's all said and done you made it to the end and graduated with

THIS IS WHY

not only a diploma but a wealth of knowledge. I have two close friends who took a little extra time to finish college. Costal Ernest who I went to high school and college with, went to several colleges as he was working toward his degree. Through all the adversity of going to different states, he finished and is living his dreams. My college friend and classmate, Tanya Simpson, also took a little longer to graduate. She graduated after transferring to multiple schools, worked full time, had a daughter, and is now working on her masters degree.

That's the kind of determination I want everyone to have. If your line isn't straight, it's ok. Create your own path and finish your goal. That's the advice I give to those who hit bumps in the road. Liad Onitoni is my friend and former intern of New Face Entertainment, Inc from New Jersey. In high school, he was at the top of his class. He wanted to go Seton Hall University in New Jersey and ended up in a six-year Pharmacy school. He could have gone to any school he wanted but "6 years 6 figures" is the phrase that persuaded him to go the college in Virginia in 2006. Moving from New Jersey to Virginia, Laid immediately associated himself with people he felt would keep him interested in staying in college. He met Taylor James, also known as DJ Tay James and the two of them joined my company. Liad eventually returned to New Jersey. Because of what he learned outside the classroom, his networking, and his ability to hustle in a positive way to be successful, he linked up with a man named Shawn Hartwell. Shawn is now a celebrity promoter and businessman in New Jersey. He isn't shy about mentioning the twenty years he spent in prison because he has used that experience to create a "whodafuckwannago2prison," helping people recognize the pitfalls of incarceration, so that they can avoid it. Liad now is the campaign manager and marketer for the campaign because of what he learned during his time leaving New Jersey. He unfortunately was unable to graduate but is able to use his skills every day. Liad could have packed it up and gave up but he decided to utilize the tools he learned while in college to make a name for himself and continue success. For Liad "6 years 6 figures" in nursing didn't happen, but the 6 figure income will.

"Despite not yet receiving my diploma. I still plan to finish my last three pre-requisite courses to get my final paperwork. It's been 6 years since my last collegiate course and the lesson I've learned the most since then, is that completion and execution are the keys to success. It's NEVER about how you start the race, and ALWAYS about how you finish it. Let nothing and no one stand in the way of your life's timeline."

-Liad Onitiri

Here is some advice to students that I have collected from college graduates who have found success in and out of the classroom.

Carrington Carter, Entrepreneur

"(1) Learning doesn't stop after college/grad school. Dedicate yourself to life-long learning. Read at least one book per month. If you want to invest wisely and build wealth, study and learn from the best who've done it.
(2) Set goals (short and long-term) for yourself, work like hell to achieve them, and chase them relentlessly.
(3) Live BELOW your means.
(4) Surround yourself with people who will push you to greatness.
(5) Maximize your time. Beware of distractions.
(6) Be aware of what you're exposing your mind to."

Jessica Mckenzie, Corporate Employee

"Never underestimate the value of internships during undergrad and graduate studies in building your skills and professional network. Yes, most of them don't pay, but the skills you gain from getting hands-on experience in your field of study is invaluable and will pay dividends when you get into the workforce. Also, remember to maintain those relationships built during those internships because some of those people can develop into your mentors and in other cases, they can provide recommendations for when you are applying for jobs. Be authentic and true to who you are. Authenticity can't be taught; people will have greater respect for you when they know who you are and what you stand for."

THIS IS WHY

Tatiani Favors, Business owner

"Advice I would give to high school students preparing for college is to really ask yourself what do you want to do, career wise, then figure out the steps to achieve that goal. If you are equipped with not only the knowledge of what you want to do, but the actual steps to achieve, you can better plan your college career. Go to college with intention and ensure the moves you make during college are reflective of your intentions. If you know you want to be in XYZ industry, then join XYZ clubs, network with people directly and indirectly related to XYZ, be on the path of achieving that goal purposefully. You must PLAN your success, it doesn't just happen by accident. Begin to try things outside of your comfort zone. Get comfortable being uncomfortable...that's where your maximum growth is! Life and experience are the best teachers. Don't be afraid to make mistakes or ask questions! Don't be afraid if your beliefs or aspirations aren't parallel to the status quo."

Shante Steward, Business Owner

"I want future students to know that it is okay to make mistakes and ask questions. College is the environment to do so. After college, people are less understanding of mistakes, especially in the workplace when you have a degree. They want you to have learned some sort of common sense in college if you did not learn it at home. Hampton and college in general is a good place to do this. Meet new people, be kind, fly like no one can bring you down, learn, breathe, scream, be joyful and try new things, but whatever you do, do it with passion and be fearless. Know, that it will all work out and trust the God of your understanding through it all. It may be cliché to say this, but what doesn't kill you, makes you stronger. That is very rule in college and throughout life! So, soak it all up in school and learn everything you can!"

THIS IS

Reginald Morris, Community leader and Business owner

"The best advice I could give to any incoming freshman is to RELAX. Everyone is awkward, nervous, and self-conscious; some are just better at masking it than others. You're going to be uncomfortable. You're going to be stretched in ways you've never imagined before. You're going to be pushed to the breaking point. It's OK to keep going. Take risks, fail, learn, and overcome. Looking back you'll be grateful for the journey. Oh and by the way… you smart enough, questionable fashion choices are a part of the college process, and there is no such thing as "black enough." We're all kings and queens."

William Y Hicks III, CPT

"Believe in yourself, never be afraid to invest in yourself and if you want to start a business the answers are on YouTube and in the library. Your success will be determined by the people you keep around you. Find you a millionaire friend who is humble. They will teach you things from a millionaires perspective about life and money management. Get a financial planner, build a portfolio and save your money for retirement. Separate yourself from negativity and trust in God."

Charles Stokes, Government Employee

"My advice to current college students is to reach out and never stop learning and growing in your craft. Reach out and reach back to those who need empowerment on and off campus. To rising High School seniors I would say research is at your fingertips. Utilize the internet and social medial properly in order for you, not your parents, to find the best pathway to education that fits nor needs and dreams. Joining organizations gives you what professionals call a "work-life" balance with cultivates a well-rounded individual. I encourage any student to join a collegiate club, organization, or divine nine organization the knowledge you will attain is immeasurable, the impact on the community is indescribable, is immeasurable and the life long friendships you make are priceless."

THIS IS WHY

Throughout these this book I mentioned various people and their experiences. I just wanted to take the time to mention a few of the people who offered their advice to let you know what they do currently.

Carrington Carter is a former big pharma brand manager turned real estate investor and serial entrepreneur who is passionate about building businesses, economic empowerment, wealth creation, and uplifting the community.

He is Co-Founder and President of McKinley Carter Enterprises, LLC (MCE) (www.McKinleyCarterEnterprises.com). MCE is a real estate investment and property management company with residential and commercial properties on Martha's Vineyard, the Pocono Mountains, Ohio, and the country of Belize, with over $5M in assets under management. The company's vacation rental homes are marketed under Getaway Society (www.GetawaySociety.com), a premium vacation rental home and travel concierge brand. "Like" his Facebook page, follow @getawaysociety on Instagram, and join his email list to stay connected.

Carrington is also Co-Founder & General Partner of East Chop Capital (www.EastChopCapital.com), a private equity firm that is currently focused on the $170 billion global vacation rental home market. Future investments will support companies in technology, financial services, media, and sports.

Prior to becoming a full-time entrepreneur, Carrington worked for 10 years in pharmaceutical marketing at Bristol-Myers Squibb, Abbott Laboratories, and inVentiv Health (now Syneos Health). Throughout his corporate career, he successfully marketed products in various stages of their life cycle, across therapeutic areas including cardiovascular disease, diabetes, antibiotics, and oncology. He gained significant experience working with diverse teams, matrix organizations, multi-million dollar budgets, and billion-dollar brands.

Carrington graduated from Hampton University with a Bachelor of Science Degree in Chemistry. He also earned an MBA in Marketing from the University of Pittsburgh Joseph M. Katz Graduate School of Business.

THIS IS

William Hicks CPT William Y Hicks III army engineer plans officer is a 16 year Captain in the Army and was Engineer Officer. He graduated from Northeastern Illinois University with a degree in Political Science. Transferred from HU as a sophomore to NEIU because of the Army. He recently received one of the highest medals an Army Engineer Officer can receive for leadership. The medal is called "The Steel Order of the de Fleury Medal" in which you have to be nominated by a Lieutenant Colonel or above. He is currently still active duty in the Army looking to retire in the next four years. He's a husband, father of two kids (boy and girl) and still host events under W. H. Productions. Currently, He does real estate investing and has a book in the production process called "Stop Selling Her a Dream" It's a self help book for young men.

Charles Stokes after graduation took various positions in criminal justice, investigations and currently employed with the Social Security Administration working as a disability examiner migrating for fraud waste and abuse of government subsidies.

Jessica Mckenzie is a Director in Global Public Policy and Government Affairs at PepsiCo. PepsiCo products are enjoyed by consumers more than one billion times a day in more than 200 countries and territories around the world, and generated more than $63 billion in net revenue in 2017. With a product portfolio that includes a wide range of enjoyable foods and beverages such as Lay's, Gatorade, Pepsi-Cola, Quaker, Tropicana, and LIFEWTR, PepsiCo generates more than $1 billion in estimated annual retail sales in 22 brands.

THIS IS WHY

Tatiani Favors is an Entrepreneur & Business Owner who graduated from the Real HU, Hampton University, in 2009 where she acquired her bachelor's degree in Accounting. She began her entrepreneurial career during college. While pursuing her Accounting degree, she fell in love with Taxation! She is a self proclaimed geek at heart! She started her first company, Sahalee Jafa Financial Services, tax preparation and bookkeeping company, by preparing family and friends tax returns for a small fee. Her passion in wanting to gain more tax preparation experience, led her to join the Volunteer Income Tax Assistance program (VITA) a volunteering program that offers free tax help to low income individuals and other taxpayers who need assistance in preparing their own tax returns. Twelve years later, Tatiani has seen every type of tax return and is extremely knowledgeable regarding both taxation and accounting for both individuals and businesses. She left Corporate America in July 2016, to focus solely on her ambitions of becoming a Business Owner & obtaining ultimate FREEDOM.

Mid-late 2017, Tatiani parted with all her accounting and bookkeeping clients because she realized, as long as she worked IN her company, she had no time to GROW her company, in order to position herself as a true Business Owner. Today, Tatiani still owns Sahalee Jafa Financial Services, LLC and is the co-owner of Thrive Tax Systems, INC., a Tax Consulting company that partners with and prepares Entrepreneurs and Self-Employed Individuals, on how to successfully run a tax preparation business.

Tatiani looks to launch two additional companies within the next couple of years while continuing to leverage and excel the two she currently oversees. Her spare time is spent with family and close friends as she has come to realize her time is more important than money. She resides in her home city of Atlanta, Ga.
Thrive Tax Systems, INC.
www.6figuretaxbusiness.com
info@thrivetaxsystems.com
"thrive tax" on all social media platforms

THIS IS

Final words
Finish what you started no matter how long it takes

"Put on your big boy pants."

My senior year of undergrad was in 2005. I was set to graduate on May 8th. Howard had graduated the year before and was in grad school at UVA. Sean had already graduated in December and told me this was his last few months with our company. I knew I didn't want work for Wall Street, even though I had an offer to do so. I felt I had something with my company and wasn't done building it. I was hosting a ballroom event and it just hit me. I didn't want to graduate and just go home. I wasn't ready. I knew it would be risky but I also knew that my mind was made up. I also knew that I had to tell my mother. Wanting to continue to build New Face Entertainment and work toward my MBA was the best way to explain it to my mother. I wanted to stay in Virginia and continue my education and business. So on this day in the middle of my event, I went into a corner behind the curtains and made the call. I call it "breaking the ice" because a phone call like that isn't going to end there. It was just the beginning of a number of discussions. But I knew at that point I was growing into myself and I was stepping into another world beyond undergrad.

As I said earlier, the degree may help you get your foot in the door but you have to sell yourself as a package and present yourself in the best way possible. And you have to deliver what you say you can. We sit on thousands of ideas and talents worth millions but end of working for peanuts compared to what we can earn.

You will have that moment of clarity at some point when you decide you are going to completely let go of your safe plans and be on your own. You spend four years of your life making your own decisions away from home. Everyone's situation is different but, for me, I was ready to make that step at graduation. Others may need to wait until it makes more economical sense; they may go home first. Either way, as I have said throughout this journey, you need a PLAN. Everyone's journey after college is different. The tools to being successful after undergrad are similar but there's a whole other level or expectations and responsibility. Take the time to consider what you need. Your plan deserves your time and attention. This is part one of a three-part series. The

THIS IS WHY

purpose of this book is to learn from me and my peers about choosing a college path and making the most of your years in college. I will go deeper into networking and life after your degree in the next two publications very soon.

For purposes of preparing for life after college, I offer a bit of advice. If I had the opportunity as my 30-year- old self to talk to my 18-year- old self, here's the first thing I would say: "Put on your big boy pants."

Think of yourself as a house. This book is a toolbox. I am giving you every tool you need to build your house. All these tools are in your toolbox.

Pay attention and read this book more than once. I would suggest reading it at least once every year to refresh and look at it as you grow into a mature young adult. Each year in college changes you as you become more and more independent growing into the person you will be for the rest of your life. There are some real gems through each section. Some tools you will use everyday to build on your house. Other tools you may only use once or twice.

Don't just read something, you have to apply it to your everyday life. You wouldn't expect to build a whole house all at once, would you? You would need to practice some skills, learn how to use the tools, and get some help sometimes. The easy part is reading the book. The hard part is applying everything in the book to your everyday life. You have the formula for success right here. Now, develop a plan and surround yourself with people who have similar goals and those who can do things you're looking to do be honest and genuine.

Use the networks that you created. Make sure you stay in contact and feed off each other. Trust me when I tell you, networking will get you a job or into graduate school faster than your degree, alone. You get paid off the value you bring, not the degree Your value is more important than the degree you receive. The degree may be what you need to get your foot in the door depending on the field you choose. That network is your family.

THIS IS

Find your strengths. Know what you do well and recognize your weaknesses. Work on them and find ways to turn those weaknesses into strengths.

Work on those intangibles constantly.

Have the unstoppable mentality. Take risks and never give up.

Create things you want to do.

Build your personal brand.

Research what you want to do in life. Set goals and write them down. Don't waste time.

Take care of your physical, mental, and spiritual health.

Give back to your community including your university in any you can. There are tax benefits as well for certain financial contributions.

Most importantly, strive to create something of your own. Whether it is a business, idea, or property. Work toward these three things: ownership, innovation and investing.

Lastly...Have Fun!

THIS IS WHY

IV. EXTRA CREDIT

This is far from over ...

THIS IS WHY YOU GO TO COLLEGE:

How to successfully graduate in REAL LIFE Studies Outside the class-room..and Beyond..

Part 2 **THIS IS WHY** YOU PREPARE FOR COLLEGE
Part 3 **THIS IS WHY** YOU NETWORK &
Part 4 **THIS IS WHY** YOU GRADUATE

Coming soon!

www.thisiswhydoc.com

Email me your success stories along the way as you utilize my

New Face Method for Success

yancy@newfacemanagement.org

I want to hear from you every step of the way!

This is the beginning of a four- part series

THIS IS

Why a book series?

In order to explain why I decided to write a book, we have to go back in time...

I, along with my best friends, Sean Washington, and Dr. Howard Crumpton, started an event planning company called Straight Face/New Face Entertainment during our freshman year in college. Sean and I went to high school together in Long Island, NY and decided to continue our education at the same institution: Hampton University. There we met Howard who was an intelligent, raw, quick-witted sophomore from Oakland, California.

Three young men with no experience, no major backing, led by only our will and ambition, created something that quickly grew to over a hundred members. This growth in membership occurred by the time I became the sole owner in 2005. New Face even offered college internship credit to help students gain meaningful experience, which often led to other opportunities for employment in related fields. Under my leadership, its members learned about small business management, financial responsibility, leadership, ownership, networking, and much more. This organization, which now has over 200 "alumni" members includes doctors, lawyers, business owners, teachers, world famous DJs, and artists. The relationships, networks, and bonds formed are unmatched. New Face also given out over $10,000 in scholarships.

I decided in the summer of 2018 to rebrand the event planning company to form New Face Management, LLC. The process started with creating a documentary based on the experiences of prior employees, associates, and interns of the company, along with the successes and failures we experienced over more than fifteen years. The documentary, called *THIS IS WHY you go to college,* is an examination of college life outside the classroom and beyond. It's an inspirational story illustrating how the things you do in college shape you into the person you will become. I began to travel across the country interviewing over a hundred business partners and friends.

The first phone call I made was to my longtime friend and former New Face Street team member, Sheronda Lawson, Esq. Sheronda graduated from Hampton University (class of 2006) and is currently an entertainment lawyer. She was the lawyer for other former members on the company who have moved on to do great things in their lives, such as DJ Tay James—Justin Bieber's official tour DJ, and Mark Jackson, award winning songwriter and producer. I felt it was an easy decision to hire Sheronda as my lawyer because of our history and her current success. Our connection was key to the early success of my company; I was her "big brother" in college and she supported New Face in its infancy with marketing and promotions. Most colleges have some variation of a big brother/big sister program where upperclassmen serve as mentors to incoming freshman. Mentors help younger students get involved in various organizations and events and get them accustomed to being a college student. Had it not been for the fact that I was a student leader and an owner of my own business at 18 years old, I would have never met Sheronda. The story of New Face Entertainment is a book in itself... stay tuned.

Fast forward to 2018. I am in the middle of filming for my documentary and have reached Hampton University Homecoming. College homecoming is a time for alumni to return to their Alma Mater for special campus events which usually includes the biggest football game of the year. I always look at Homecoming as a big network reunion.It not only gives you a weekend to reminisce about your college days, see old friends that live all over the world, and reconnect with people you haven't seen in a while it gives the opportunity every year to make network with people now who live all over the world creating more opportunity to build business and personal relationships.

Homecoming every year opens opportunities for business connections and potential leads for the future. It's one big network of people that share the experience of having gone to the same college. During Hampton University's Homecoming of 2018, Sheronda and I hosted the first "In the Industry" panel. We had Alumni from different aspects of the entertainment industry giving their perspective on their jobs and offering advice for those interested in going into similar positions. It felt good to be able to still give back to college students and pass on a message through the eyes of multiple graduates. Plus, it provided an opportunity for students and alumni to connect and learn more about what Hampton students do after graduation. An "In the Industry" panel was held to allow students and alumni from 1999-2018 to network and find out what it took to be successful in their respective fields.

Our expectation was for students to be inspired by alumni and consider ways to make the path easier for reaching their personal goals. The event was very successful with great engagement even during a peak time of Homecoming on a rainy day in October. Our panel was diverse with many different perspectives. Students and alumni were able to network and get a better understanding of many things that are often overlooked when talking about the industry.

Justin Sharpe, a college student from Baltimore, MD, provided filming and photography for the event. As a college student himself, he was able to network with people twice his age and gain opportunities with alumni he might have never been able to meet otherwise. That was the point of the seminar.

On the panel, we had Olympic medalists, worldwide DJs, entrepreneurs, business owners, heads of corporate companies, lawyers, etc.

As the function went on, I began to think about how everything was created and why people were in support of the event. It had nothing to do with the degrees everyone had in the room. People barely mentioned what their majors were. The focus was on what they had done to maximize achievement while in college outside the classroom, and how those things affected their current careers. Don't get me wrong-degrees are important and are needed in many endeavors no matter the field of study. The degree is recognized before any-thing else to get a foot in the door and shows that a candidate is capable of learning. However, there is more worth in what can be learned outside the classroom, which is a *degree* in itself. Had it not been for the network, the ability to talk to people, and the relationships built over the years in college, people would not have been interested in listening to the panelist. Each of them owed their success-at least in part-to the knowledge they gained outside the classroom.

Following the success of the event, I decided to take time off from working on the documentary to figure out how to illustrate the power in having a network. I wanted to demonstrate the impact of developing the skills of communication, networking, persuasion, and motivation. Of course, not everyone can develop into a master motivator/business owner/people person. THIS IS WHY I decid-ed to write a series of books creating a pathway of success for those looking for the answers to a test we already passed.

THIS IS WHY

Although there is no physical diploma you receive for everything that is done in college outside the classroom, the knowledge and experience you can receive is unmatched. The degree you receive in the classroom will have more worth if you take advantage of everything college has to offer outside of the classroom.

Few have mastered the art of turning an idea into a function people would want to attend. Even fewer possess the skill to monetize such an event. People need to learn how to develop this skill and create their own. Part of my personal legacy is passing this knowledge down to others. This series begins that important transfer for information. I will follow it up with seminars and tutorials on being successful outside the classroom.

For footage of the event and a list of the panelists, feel to go to my website www.newfacemanagement.org.

THIS IS

About the Author

James Yancy Merchant, Jr. is the owner of New Face Management, LLC and creator of Success Without Limitations.

Originally from Queens, New York, Yancy was a scholar student and talented athlete. His childhood and adolescent years would provide a series of opportunities to gain interest in both the business and event planning industry. Upon graduation from high school, he and best friend Sean Washington committed to attending a historically black college noting its prominence in academia and culture would introduce these young men to a new world of possibilities. Both young men were accepted into the prestigious institution of Hampton University with the intention of developing into young, successful entrepreneurs within the Hampton Roads area. As thriving, full-time students in exceptional academic standing, Merchant and Washington soon befriended fellow scholar Dr. Howard Crumpton and the three would establish the promotional company Straight face Entertainment. Later Mr. Merchant became the sole owner of the company known as New Face Entertainment, Inc.

New Face became more than a profitable company; it evolved into a movement. As their network increased in size and quality, New Face hosted more than on and off campus events. As a company, New Face empowered college students and alumni socially, professionally, emotionally and mentally. New Face provided over $10,000 in scholarships and donations towards student organizations, created numerous internship opportunities for students in their respective fields, sponsored athletic events, hosted mental health seminars, initiated beautification projects, offered tutoring services, donated food and clothing to homeless shelters and so much more.

While managing New Face, Merchant created the community-based component of the company, Success Without Limitations. Presently, he is expanding SWL, rebranded now known as New Face to New Face Management, LLC doing management consulting. He is also the creator, director, and producer of *This is Why*, a series documenting a historical reflection of college life outside the classroom and beyond set to release in 2019. Merchant is also a proud father. He works for the city of New York and is developing a series of memoirs on the breadth, journey, and lessons learned from his life and experience in the entertainment business. THIS IS WHY..

THIS IS WHY

Sean Washington, Co-founder of Straight Face Entertainment

Sean Washington is a results-oriented business professional who excels in attracting, retaining, deepening and developing business relationships. As a Senior Business Development Manager in the Economic Development Department in the city of Norfolk, Virginia, Sean is responsible for the administration of capital access programs that assist with the start-up, growth, and expansion of businesses in the City of Norfolk. Sean also serves as the Assistant Executive Director and Secretary/Treasurer for the Economic Development Authority for the City of Norfolk.

Raised in Long Island New York, Sean became a member of the Hampton Roads community as a Business Administration student at Hampton University. During his undergraduate tenure, he served as president of the New York Pre-Alumni Association and the Entrepreneurship Club. He was also a member of the OFVC Entrepreneurship Invitational Business Plan Team and The Society of Business Professionals. His entrepreneurial spirit led to the co-creation of the promotional company "New Face Entertainment," which created a lasting mark on campus activities.

Sean began his professional career as a financial representative for American General Finance, a subsidiary of AIG. There, he had the responsibility of personal and real estate lending, monitoring delinquent accounts and proposing financing options to retail dealers. His efforts not only raised the branch's overall lending volume from $14 to $15 million, but a 10% profit gain was recognized from 2007-2008. In 2011, Sean expanded his finance and lending experience by being selected into the BB&T Leadership Development Program, which resulted in his previous title of Assistant Vice President at BB&T Bank. As a small business lender and market leader, Sean was responsible for managing a $34.5 million deposit portfolio and a $15 million lending portfolio.

Sean balances his passion for helping small businesses thrive while giving countless hours of his time to the community. He's a board member of Parents Against Bullying VA, previously served as president of the Urban League of Hampton Roads Young Professionals, and was co-chair for BB&T's Multicultural Committee during his tenure with the bank. Sean has also volunteered with the Cystic Fibrosis Foundation, Roc Solid Organization, I-THRive mentoring program, Toastmasters International, and Norfolk's Bank-on Your Success Program, where he assists individuals and families reach their financial goals. He is also the Assistant Department Head of the Sound Ministry at Full Gospel Kingdom Church. Sean spends his downtime reading, exercising, and traveling with his wife, Jessica Larche Washington.

One of Sean's favorite quotes is "Don't let your charisma take you somewhere your character can't keep you." Sean's integrity, hard work and faithfulness to both his career and community are evidence of his highly respected character. He looks forward to building a legacy of service and growth for years to come.

Dr. Howard Crumpton, PhD Co-founder of Straight face Entertainment

Howard Crumpton, PhD is the owner and CEO of Reach Out Therapy, LLC. Dr. Crumpton earned his Ph.D. in Clinical Psychology from the Curry School of Education at the University of Virginia. His clinical internship, with specialties rotations in Adolescent Medicine and Bilingual Assessment, was completed at Children's Hospital Los Angeles, a part of the University of Southern California University Center on Excellence in Developmental Disabilities.

Upon completion of his doctoral degree, Dr. Crumpton spent two years as a postdoctoral fellow at the Kennedy Krieger Institute within the Johns Hopkins University School of Medicine in Maryland. There, he trained in the Behavior Management and Child and Family Therapy clinics, providing multi-systemic support to parents, medical professionals, and educators in addressing emotional, behavioral, social, and academic problems in children and adolescents. Dr. Crumpton served as a Spanish-English bilingual staff psychologist and key contributor to the development of the Primary Care Behavioral Health Services at the Children's National Health System, where he provided family focused therapy, assessment and behavioral health consultations in collaboration with medical professionals within and outside the hospital system. He has also served as a psychological evaluator at The MECCA Group, LLC, a private practice in Washington, D.C. owned and operated by women of color. Dr. Crumpton currently provides mental health and consultative services for families as a family psychologist at Encore Recovery Services in Arlington, VA, a substance recovery startup that provides young adults and their families with holistic cutting-edge services to address substance addiction and co-occurring mental health disorders.

While Dr. Crumpton's target population includes all children, he holds particular interests in treating such concerns in the Latino community with families whose primary language is Spanish. His demonstrated research interests include increasing motivation and academic success of low-achieving students, the impact of warm and supportive teacher-student interactions on student classroom behavior, and the psychological assessment of culturally and linguistically diverse student populations.

Dr. Crumpton currently resides in the Washington, DC area with his wife and three children. In his spare time, Dr. Crumpton plays the drums, learns new languages, travels with his family, and plays video games.

THIS IS

About New Face Management, LLC

New Face Management, LLC is a management consulting company that supports business and organizations by developing a strategy to become successful through networking and proper planning. The mission is to give knowledge on how to expand your network and grow your business providing and exceptional network to college students, alumni, and entrepreneurs bridging the communication gap in our community.

New Face Management, LLC originated from New Face Entertainment, INC. which was an event planning company, formed in 2005 in Hampton Roads ,VA first as Straight Face Entertainment. New Face Ent. endeavored to serve college students and organizations across the Hampton Roads area, creating weekly events such as cabarets, dance competitions, student center events, and social gatherings. New Face served as a safe haven for students to enjoy themselves outside of the classroom with events that catered specifically to the needs of college students. The majority of New FACE's members attended the historically black college (HBCU), Hampton University. This team of student entrepreneurs began with three members in 2001, later expanding to over 100 members in 2005. The entertainment company even offered college internship credit as a means of gaining authentic experience which often lead to future employment in related fields. Under the leadership of its owner, James Yancy Merchant, its members learned about small business management, financial responsibility, leadership , ownership, networking and much more. This organization, which now has over 200 "alumni" members, includes doctors, lawyers, business owners, teachers, world renowned DJs and artists. The relationships, networks and bonds formed are unmatched.

For more information on the company's services visit :

www.newfacemanagement.org

THIS IS WHY

THIS IS WHY DOCUMENTARY

During the 2006-2007 academic year, footage was recorded of all meetings, events, and social gatherings of the company. The trials and tribulations of balancing academic expectations and a growing business were all documented from hundreds of hours of raw footage. This footage showcases thousands of college students enjoying a pivotal time in their college careers.

In 2018, Mr. Merchant traveled across the country to various states in the U. S. including New York, Virginia, Maryland, Nevada, and California as well as Washington, DC to interview more than a hundred past members about what was once, arguably, the best college event planning company on the East Coast. These interviews were used for a documentary called *This is Why: A Historical Reflection of College Life Outside the Classroom*. The *This is Why* documentary will showcase the history and journey of New Face Entertainment over a fifteen-year period and the effect its existence had on the city, its members, supporters, interns, and scholarship recipients.

This documentary inspires our youth in high school to consider college as both a means for continuing to learn and expand one's education and a way of connecting, growing, and making their dreams a reality. We have built a network of over 3 million followers on social media. There was a time when all of these people were together in one city following a collective mission to make college enjoyable and fun. Although we are now scattered across the world as successful adults, the commonality that is New Face Entertainment still binds us. College is as much about getting a degree as it is about building relationships, stepping out the box, testing the limits of one's abilities, and growing into adults with a unique perspective on life. This documentary will define the WHY in the phrase *THIS IS WHY You Go to College.*

For more information on the documentary visit

www.thisiswhydoc.com

THIS IS

Success Without Limitations

In 2004, through New Face Entertainment, Mr. Merchant put a name to the various community service ventures done as a company called Success Without Limitations. An assortment of college students applied and received financial scholarships. Student organizations such as Fraternities and Sororities receive monetary donations in the thousands. Seminars about suicide and depression were held by SWL. Campus beautification projects were planned and executed like the repaving of basketball courts on the campus of Hampton University. SWL also sponsored various youth sports teams, donated to battered women's shelters, and participated in food drives for less fortunate families. In 2007, as a graduate student, James Yancy Merchant along with undergraduate students on the campus of Old Dominion University created the student organization SWL (Success Without Limitations) which is still active today with over 200 members.

The purpose of SWL is to create a culturally friendly environment through educational, social, and community programming, which will develop leadership and civility among our members. We will strive to accomplish our purpose though the co-sponsorship of campus events, extensive community service, family-oriented projects, and campus beautification. Success Without Limitations will bridge the gap between what is learned in the classroom in college and what is learned outside the classroom such as dealing with anxiety, depression, social gatherings as a young adult, and preparing for the conflicts college students may face. Students will also have the opportunity to gain internships through the organization strong ties to the community and alumni.

We are looking to expand Success Without Limitations to high schools and colleges across the country. We want YOU to be a part of the movement.

Contact SuccessWithoutLimitations2005@gmail.com to start an SWL chapter at your high school or college:

https://www.newfacemanagement.org/success-without-limitations/

THIS IS WHY

Motivation

Often, people come into your life for reasons you may not understand until much later in life. I regard Dr. Shaun Woodly as an advisor. He is also my fraternity big brother, he worked for me as a DJ, and we served as the groomsmen in each other's weddings. I met Shaun when I made the decision to become a brother of the Gamma Iota Chapter of Alpha Phi Alpha Fraternity, Inc. in 2003. I have always respected and admired him. A native of Long Island, NY, he was a member of a band, played the drums, held the position of drum major, and was the *Candyman Step Master* for our fraternity chapter. Fast forward to 2006, we both decided to become educators in the Hampton Roads area. However, Shaun also decides to become a DJ. He had very compelling reasons for these decisions that you will learn when you watch the documentary.

Our friendship and fraternal bond grew as my company grew. Presently, Dr. Woodly is a husband, father of two, professor, podcast owner, and author of the newly released book, *MC Means Moved the Class* (available on Amazon). His success motivated me to do more to change the world. He remained focused on his goal and achieved great things. I was so impressed, I was compelled to step up my own game.

I might have never met Shaun in a college classroom. I met him because I pledged a fraternity. From there, our relationship blossomed through shared business aspirations and a determination to make a difference in the community.

Coach Bill Mitaritonna is my former high school varsity head basketball coach. During his first year as a head coach at Half Hollow Hills West, I was one of four of his chosen captains. You wonder what a high school coach has to do with this? You are going to have to wait for the full story. But I'll just say now that, although we are about ten years apart, we both went to the same private school in Rosedale. Neither of us were the best players, but we both positively impacted our teams. We were both teachers, and he helped me raise the money I needed when I started New Face working for him during the summer. He goes down in history of one of the greatest coaches in Long Island. He recently published his memoir, *Last of the Redmen*, (available on Amazon) He is now one of my book coaches and is featured on the *This is Why* documentary.

THIS IS

Tamra Sease has been my editor since I turned event planning into a business. She was an English major in college and helped edit the majority of my business proposals and letters. She currently inspires me as my coach and my editor for personal work and for business. She is one of the most reliable people I know, and I have trusted her with confidential business information for years. Tamra has now released multiple books (available on Amazon) and dedicated her time to help me with my first publication.

Lastly, my children motivate me to be the best person I could be. The way they look to me everyday to guide them and show them the way to life motivates me to be better and do better. My children force me to be responsible – to be a man of my word. There is no way I can say or do anything without them holding me accountable. They watched me work on this everyday, and I refused to let them see me fail.

THIS IS WHY

Afterward

Be humble and grateful to be in the position you are in. My grandmother and my mother always said there is always someone who would kill to be in the position you are in.

Please support the Preparatory book to this series *This Is WHY you prepare for College. ...by making the right choice for YOU coming this fall !*

THIS IS WHY you go to college is the first of a four-part publication. The third publication will go deeper into the "Power of the Network" through the history of New Face called THIS IS WHY YOU NETWORK &
Part four THIS IS WHY YOU GRADUATE will focus on using the skills you learned through my method outside of the classroom AFTER graduation showing how life is truly a business.

Sign up for my email list at www.thisiswhydoc.com for release dates.

THIS IS

Suggested reading material and references

7 Habits of Highly Effective People, by Stephen Covey
Think and Grow Rich by Napoleon Hill
MC Means Move the Class, by Shaundau Woodly, Ph.D.
The Secret, by Rhonda Byrne
Last of the Redmen, by Bill Mitaritonna
Engaging Children in Learning: The Extracurricular Academics Model, by
Dotteanna k. Garlington, Ed.d.
History of the Black Dollar, by Angel Rich
Published, by Chandler Bolt
Mixed Emotions, by Andrew Nguyen and Pauleanna Reid
SOL Affirmations: A Tool Kit for Reflection and Manifesting the Light Within,
by Karega Bailey
You Got Into Where? How I Received Admission and Scholarships to the Na-
tion's Top Universities by Joi Wade
Guide me to college: 10 vital steps every urban youth need for college by Starr
Essence

Suggested Viewing

"We are rising" is a documentary where you learn about HBCUs and their rich
history Available on Netflix
THIS IS WHY you go to college documentary interviews can be viewed at
www.thisiswhydoc.com

Know Yourself Assessment
"Your perception is your reality."

Even if you know these answers, I want you literally write them down. It's much different to see them organized on paper. Use extra paper if you need it.

What do you want to do after you graduate College?

_____

_____

_____

What charges you up? What are you interested in every day?

_____

_____

_____

What makes you happy?

_____

_____

_____

What are your goals?

_____

_____

_____

What is your definition of success?

_____

_____

_____

How can going to college help you be successful and achieve your goals?

_____

_____

_____

THIS IS

What is your current network?

_____

_____

_____

Do you need your network to grow in order to achieve your goals?

_____

_____

_____

Thank you to all those who took the time to help put this publication together.
Your input has been invaluable.

First Name	Last Name	Instagram Contact
Andrew	Bisnaught	@babeydrew
Angel	Rich	@angelrich27
Anika	Willams	@nika_denelle
Anwar (DJ SUAVE)	Miles	@djsuave1963
Bianca	Campbell	@binka629
Bill	Mitaritonna	@lastoftheredmen
Blake	Kelly	@blakekelly
Booker	Forte	@bookerforte
Brandon	Taylor	@ayience_fitness
Broadway	Chapman	@pictureb
Bruce	Brown	@brucelbrown0701
Carl	Gray III	@graymatta
Caron	Washington	@kappatalize
Carrington	Carter	@carringtonmcarter
Charles	Stokes	@thediplomat06
Chris	Cardwell	@i_am_goodnews
Chris	Roy	@chris_roy
Christopher	Queen	@frostbyte07
Clay	West	@mrwestmrfresh
Coastal	Ernest	@coach_cos1

THIS IS

Conrad	Llewellyn	@flyfinefocused
Crystal	Neal	@hampton_terps
Danna	Merchant	@dm_merch1040
Day'nah	Cooper-Evans	@iamdaynah
Derrick	Taylor	@custom_taylored
Devin	Green	@officialdevingreen
Dominique	Wilkins	@_domoniquenatasha
Dotti	Garlington	@callmedoctor_18
Dr. Brian	Mcclure,PHD	@bmcclure2
Dr. Byron	Mcclure, Ded	@bmcclure6
Dr. Howard	Crumpton, PhD	n/a
Dr. Shaun	Woodly, PHD	@shaundau
Dr.Timothy	Fraizer, MD	@skilledhands_gifted-heart
Edwin	Mcclure	@mygreatcomeback
Ellen	Dunn	n/a
Fresh	Redding	@freshredding
Gavin	McEachin	@young_gav
Ian	Brown	@walt_thizzney
J'vonn	Forbes	@iamjforbes
James	Callaham	@elcapitanambassador
Jayee	Person-Lynn, Esq	@lincolnlawyerla
Jenar	Harrison	@Allaboutdot
Jessica	Gordon-Mckenzie	n/A

THIS IS WHY

Joseph	Walters	@hb1network
Joshua	Estrada	@westmoments
Jovan	Brown	@joaudacity
Justin	Sharpe	@justcobar
Karega	Bailey	@karegabailey
Karmia	Berry	@karmiaberry
Karson	Austin	@kingaustin4
Keion	Mcdaniels	@mymainman_keion
Kellie	Wells	@kelliewellsbrinkley
Khaleel	Artist	@k.artis
Kiira	Harper	@kiiraharper
Laquan	Stewart	n/A
Liad	Onitiri	@kingputon
Mark	Jackson	@markthemogul
Marquis	Dennis	@theartofabs
Marvin	Ganthier	@djmarvalous
Matthew	White	@gingerkid85
Michelle	Rodgers	@michellenicole87
Mimi	Wilson	@nailsbymimi
Monet	Clements	N/A
Mya	Brooks	@flyyfree_myab
Nickolas	Mitchell	@nickluvin4
Nikki	Walker	@imapo3t
Norschon	Sheridan	@thechampagnegang
Paul	Saunders	@passportps

THIS IS

Phil	Smith	@philthedjlp
Rachel	Preston	n/a
Reggie	Morris	@djregyreg
Rev. Mike	Wortham	@michaelswortham
Rob	Rich	@_robrich
Ryan	Marsh	@ryankmarsh
Sean	Gaddy	n/a
Sean	Washington	@seanmwashington
Shante Alesia	Stewart	@shantealesia
Shatera	Smith	@dishea222
Sheronda	Lawson, Esq	@shaymlawson
Sianni	Caballo	@siannijessica
Stan	Wyatt	@stan_the3rd
Tamra	Sease	@tamsease
Tanya	Simpson	@thedreamgirlbrand
Tatiani	Favors	@tatianifavors
Taylor	James	@djtayjames
Traci	Steele	@tracisteele
Travon	Williams	@travonwlms
Tyrell	Clay	@flavaice_
Tyrique	Taylor	@fynaflo
Victor	Rogers	@ceo_vic357
Vincint	Hancock	@djvince757
Wakita	Taylor	@wakilee
William	Hicks, CPT	@integrityisallyouhave

THIS IS WHY

THIS IS

247

THIS IS WHY

THIS IS

THIS IS WHY

THIS IS

THIS IS WHY

THIS IS

THIS IS WHY

THIS IS

THIS IS WHY

THIS IS

Made in the USA
Monee, IL
30 November 2019